No Place To Stand Alone

No Place To Stand Alone

**Historical Mergers and Acquisitions
in Different Corporate Markets**

Ashraf Haggag

ISBN-13: 9781541353084
ISBN-10: 1541353080

Contents

One   Introduction. 1
Two   The Challenges of Competition in
               Various Market Sectors 3
Three   Definition of Mergers and Acquisitions . . . 6
Four   Types of Mergers 8
Five   Why Companies Merge with or
               Acquire Other Companies 11
Six   Why Mergers and Acquisitions Fail. 14

Mergers and Acquisitions in the
Pharmaceutical Field · **19**
Seven   Pharmaceutical Mergers and
               Acquisitions. 21
Eight   Glaxo Wellcome and SmithKline
               Beecham Merger. 26
Nine   Pfizer and Wyeth Acquisition 30
Ten   Pfizer and Warner-Lambert Acquisition . . 34
Eleven   Aventis and Sanofi Merger 38

Twelve   Actavis and Allergan Acquisition 42
Thirteen   Merck and Schering-Plough Merger. 46

Mergers and Acquisitions in the Airline Industry· · · · · 51
Fourteen   Mergers and Acquisitions in the
              Airline Industry 53
Fifteen   Emirates and Qantas Partnership 58
Sixteen   British Airways and Iberia Merger. 62
Seventeen   Lufthansa Acquisition of Swiss Air 66
Eighteen   Air France and KLM Merger 71
Nineteen   Etihad Airways and Air Berlin Partnership . . . 75

**Mergers and Acquisitions in the
Hospitality Industry · 79**
Twenty   Mergers and Acquisitions in the
              Hospitality Industry. 81
Twenty-One   Accor Acquisition of Fairmont
              Raffles Hotels International 86
Twenty-Two   IHG Group Acquisition of Kimpton
              Hotel and Restaurant Group. 90
Twenty-Three Marriott Acquisition of Starwood 94

Mergers and Acquisitions in the Oil Sector · · · · · · · · · 99
Twenty-Four   Mergers and Acquisitions in the
              Oil Sector 101
Twenty-Five   Exxon and Mobil Merger 106
Twenty-Six   British Petroleum and Amoco
              Oil Merger. 110

Mergers and Acquisitions in the Retail &
Services Field ···································**115**

Twenty-Seven   Mergers and Acquisitions in the
                Retail & Services Field. 117
Twenty-Eight   Facebook Acquisition of WhatsApp. . . . 120
Twenty-Nine   Kraft and Heinz Merger. 123
Thirty   AOL and Time Warner Merger 127
Thirty-One   Vodafone Acquisition of Mannesmann. . 132
Thirty-Two   Mars and Wrigley Acquisition 137
Thirty-Three   Procter and Gamble Acquisition
                of Gillette 141
Thirty-Four   Philip Morris Acquisition of Nabisco
                Holdings Corp. 145
Thirty-Five   Kraft Foods and Cadbury Acquisition . . .149
Thirty-Six   Nestlé and Gerber Acquisition 153
Thirty-Seven   PepsiCo and Tropicana Acquisition 157
Thirty-Eight   Adidas acquisition of Reebok 161
Thirty-Nine   Coca-Cola and Glacéau Vitaminwater
                Acquisition. 165
Forty   Microsoft's Acquisition of Nokia 169
Forty-One   Royal Bank of Scotland Consortium
                Acquisition of ABN AMRO 174
Forty-Two   Conclusions About Mergers and
                Acquisitions. 179

About the Author 183

One

Introduction

Hello, I am Ashraf Haggag. I am writing this book primarily for my two kids, Abdullah and Abdul Rahman. They have not progressed in their careers yet, and since they both wish to be in the business and management fields when they graduate, I thought of giving them the most valuable lesson in management: how to handle challenges that each day brings.

How, when you are on the top of an organization facing cutthroat competition, do you think out of the box and come up with ideas and create new market zones for your company that not only ensures stability in the market but also achieves a leap in your organization's performance?

I hadn't thought for one minute that I could write a book one day, but I am a top, senior executive with years of experience spent in diversified operational and managerial capacities among landmark, international, hospitality corporations. My previous experience has allowed me to be very close to the corporate market and to witness all major upturns and downturns of its different fields, such as pharmaceuticals, banking, oil and gas, and aviation.

This accumulated past experience has given me the courage to formulate and put forward business thoughts based on different case studies that took place within various international corporations. These are companies that have overcome challenges and created new market space when competition was at its peak.

I hope the accumulation of these business thoughts put together as a book can be not only a guideline to academic students but also as a road map for companies facing cutthroat competition, whether they are start-up companies or a well-established ones.

Enjoy the read.

Two

The Challenges of
Competition in Various
Market Sectors

Competition is rapidly growing in various market sectors, and a strong trend has developed of mergers and acquisitions among corporate companies creating huge organizations that add more pressure and competitive environments. Managers and top executives must understand their company's competitive advantage and build strategies that take into account the competitive landscape.

The following elements and factors should be taken into deep consideration and attention.

COMPETITIVE STRATEGIES
From a managerial prospective, competition generally falls into the external environment, although it can also take shape in internal environment, through rivalry between strategic-business units for managers. Understanding the external competitive landscape is a critical factor in assessing

company strategies and benchmarking appropriately to ensure competitiveness.

Businesses that fail to keep pace with their rivals will eventually be overpowered and often forced to develop an exit strategy.

Avoiding the risks of competitive factors requires a strong understanding of operational efficiency, quality production, differentiation, and competitive advantage.

LOW COSTS AND BRANDING

The simplest perspective in competition is in industries where products are homogeneous. In such situations, companies compete directly. For example, bottled-water producers are directly involved in such a framework and thus adopt two basic competitive strategies: low costs and branding.

Low-cost suppliers find ways to optimize their production and distribution to offer consumers the lowest-possible price on one bottle of water; low-cost suppliers often benefit largely from economies of scale. Branding, on the other hand, aims to convince the consumer that a higher price point is worth paying based upon the company's name, reputation, or other distinguishing characteristics.

DIFFERENTIATION

Most products and services are not homogeneous; however, they allow incumbents in an industry to compete with one another by means of various competitive strategies. Differentiation is a competitive tactic wherein companies approach certain niche needs within an industry to capture a segment of the market share.

QUALITY

There is the potential to compete externally based upon quality. For example, Toyota produces both the Corolla and Lexus, thereby targeting both ordinary automobile drivers and those in the luxury-car consumer bracket. Strategies related to branding provide a particular level of quality to capture a specific income or a specific level of clientele. The opportunity cost of efficiency is associated with quality, which generally sees higher price points. Quality is therefore a strong antithesis to the low-cost strategy.

INTERNAL COMPETITION

Businesses also compete internally. An intrinsically complex issue, on the surface, internal competition involves either direct product substitute or funding competition. For example, PepsiCo produces both colas and sport drinks, all of which sit on the shelf next to one another.

When a customer sees the sports drink and chooses it over the cola option, the cola has lost a sale to an internal competitor. The mother company (i.e. PepsiCo), however, did not lose a sale; it merely lost one segment of the business while gaining another.

With these points in mind, managers must thoroughly understand the products they are pitching and the strategy that will help them avoid going head-to-head with other businesses with which they cannot compete.

Three

Definition of Mergers and Acquisitions

Although "mergers" and "acquisitions" are often used as synonymous terms, there are differences between the two concepts. These differences follow.

MERGERS

Two firms together form a new company; after they merge, the separately owned companies become jointly owned and obtain a new single identity. The stock of both companies is surrendered and new stocks in the name of the new company are issued.

Mergers usually take place between two companies of more or less the same size. In these cases, the process is called "mergers of equals."

ACQUISITIONS

One company takes over another company and establishes its power as the single owner. The company that takes over is usually the bigger and stronger in terms of financial capability.

The company that takes over runs the whole business with its own identity; stocks of the acquired company are not sur-rendered but bought by the public prior to the acquisition and continue to be traded on the stock market.

Four

Types of Mergers

Mergers and acquisitions can be categorized according to the nature of the merger. Hence, it is important to differentiate and understand the subtle differences as follows.

CONGLOMERATE MERGER

A conglomerate merger is a merger between firms that are involved in totally unrelated business activities. There are two types of conglomerate mergers. The first is a pure conglomerate merger, which involves firms with nothing in common. The second is a mixed conglomerate merger, which involves firms that are looking for product extensions or market extension.

EXAMPLE

A manufacturer of athletic shoes merges with a soft-drink firm. The resulting new company will be faced with the same competition in each of its two markets after the merger as the individual firms were before the merger. A clear case of conglomerate merger is the Walt Disney Company and the

American Broadcasting Company, whereby both were working in totally different markets with different competition.

HORIZONTAL MERGER

A horizontal merger takes place between companies in the same industry and field; it is a sort of consolidation that occurs between firms operating in the same market facing the same competition and market conditions and offering same products or services. Horizontal mergers are common in industries with fewer firms, when competition tends to be tense and synergies and potential gains are much greater.

EXAMPLE

In a merger between Coca-Cola and PepsiCo's Pepsi beverage division, the goal would be to create a new, larger, and stronger organization with a greater market share.

MARKET-EXTENSION MERGER

A merger takes place between two companies that deal in the same products but in separate markets. The main purpose of such a merger is to make sure that merging companies can get access to a larger market and a bigger client base as well.

EXAMPLE

An example of a market extension merger is the acquisition of Eagle Bancshares, Inc. by RBC Centura. Eagle Bancshares, Inc. is headquartered at Atlanta, Georgia and has 283 workers. It has almost 90,000 accounts and looks after assets worth US $1.1 billion. Eagle Bancshares also holds the Tucker

Federal Bank, which is one of the ten biggest banks in the metropolitan Atlanta region as far as deposit market share is concerned. One of the major benefits of this acquisition is that this acquisition enables the RBC to go ahead with its growth operations in the North American market. With the help of this acquisition RBC gained the chance to deal in the financial market of Atlanta, which was among the leading up-coming financial markets in the USA. This move allowed RBC to diversify its base of operations.

PRODUCT-EXTENSION MERGER

A product-extension merger takes place between two business organizations that deal in products related to each other and operate in the same field. It allows the merging companies to group their products together and get access to a bigger set of customers.

EXAMPLE

The acquisition of Mobilink Telecom Inc. by Broadcom is a proper example of the product extension merger. Broadcom deals in the manufacturing Bluetooth personal area network hardware systems and chips for IEEE 802.11b wireless LAN. While Mobilink Telecom Inc. deals in the manufacturing of product designs meant for handsets that are equipped with the Global System for Mobile Communications technology. Therefore the products of Mobilink Telecom Inc. perfectly complement the wireless products of Broadcom.

Five

Why Companies Merge with or Acquire Other Companies

Companies grow in mainly two ways, either they grow organically or merge with / acquire other companies. Nowadays, the trend of acquiring existing companies has never been greater to the extent that it has become the norm within the corporate world. This route is a fast way to reshape corporate strategy and get access to markets, products, technologies and managerial talents. Below, you will find and understand the reasons behind mergers and acquisitions.

SYNERGY
One of the major reasons for a merger or acquisition is synergy. Synergy is the combination of business activities in order to improve performance either financially (decrease and control operational costs) and or the quality of the final product.

DIVERSIFICATION AND SHARPENING OF BUSINESS FOCUS

These two conflicting goals have been used to describe thousands of mergers and acquisitions. A company that merges to diversify may acquire another company in a seemingly unrelated industry in order to reduce the impact of a particular industry's performance on its profitability.

Companies seeking to sharpen focus often merge with other companies that have deeper and stronger market penetration in a key area of operation.

GROWTH

Mergers can give the acquiring companies opportunity to grow a market share without having to really earn it by doing the work themselves. Instead they buy a competitor's business for a price.

For example, a pharmaceutical company may choose to buy out a smaller competing company in order to enable the smaller company to produce more and sell more due to its brand-loyal customers.

INCREASING SUPPLY-CHAIN PRICING POWER

When a company is buying out one of its suppliers, the company will be able to save on the margins that the supplier was previously adding to its cost. This will enable the acquiring company to be more aggressive and competitive in terms of pricing among its competitors.

ELIMINATING COMPETITION

Many merger or acquisition deals lead to the elimination of future competition and thus enable the company to gain a larger market share within the market of its products. The downside of this is that a large premium is usually required to convince the acquiring company's (company doing the buying) shareholders to accept the offer.

Six

Why Mergers and Acquisitions Fail

Markets have witnessed a sudden leap in mergers and acquisitions. In the year 2008–2009, approximately five thousand eight hundred companies were involved in the process of merger and acquisition, which accounted for nearly $2.3 trillion.

Recent trends show that many companies have opted for either a merger or an acquisition without conducting proper due diligence. Mergers and acquisitions may help the parent company in increasing its market share, lowering the cost of production, increasing competitiveness, and improving profit. But contrary to popular perception, this is not always the case. Many cases have been seen in which the merger and acquisition have not been able to produce the required results.

A high percentage of mergers and acquisitions fail, as companies are not able to set and meet their targets. The major reasons as to why mergers and acquisitions fail can be explained as follows.

OVERESTIMATING THE VALUE OF THE TARGET COMPANY

The basic aim of a company in a merger and acquisition is to provide benefits and return of investment to the shareholders. However, in reality, most of the companies are not able to achieve this, and so many examples show that many parent companies often overestimate the value of their target company due to lack of due diligence.

EXAMPLE

An example of this is the Daimler-Benz and Chrysler group. In 1998, the German auto car maker Daimler-Benz merged with Chrysler group for a value of $36 billion. It was considered to be a win-win situation for both companies. However, after a few years, the value of Chrysler fell by $7.4 billion, and that was because Daimler-Benz never conducted a proper due diligence before it merged with Chrysler. In other words, it overestimated the value of the targeted company, which led to an unsuccessful merger.

HIGH-COST DEBT

Many times the acquirer gets submerged in large and extraordinary debts during mergers and acquisitions. Most transactions are financed through unsecured debts, which carry a huge rate of interest with them. These high-cost debts eventually lead to a fail in the stock price of the parent company. When two or more companies bid for the same company, they may end up paying more than the target company.

EXAMPLE

In 2008, Tata Motors acquired Jaguar. All the analysts confirmed that it was Tata's ambition to become a global company in a short time. Since a very high cost was paid, the deal was financed by Tata through a high-cost debt. Later on, shareholders of both companies suffered a huge blow as Tata tried to raise money to cover this huge acquisition debt.

JOB LOSSES

One of the major reasons why mergers and acquisitions fail is the fear among the employees about job losses. According to statistics, approximately one hundred thirty thousand jobs have been lost as a result of mergers and acquisitions in the European financial sector over the past 15 years. The job loss is mainly the result of the company going into cost-cutting strategies to give more breathing space to its financial balance sheet.

EXAMPLES

In the merger between Chemical Bank and Chase Manhattan in 1995, nearly twelve thousand jobs were eliminated.

When National Bank was acquiring Bank of America in 1998, it included plans to lay off nearly eighteen thousand employees.

CULTURAL ASPECTS

This is one of the biggest challenges that companies face during mergers and acquisitions. As no two companies can perform the same way, the working environment and organization culture of every company is different, in terms of the way the companies project themselves on the market and deal with customers, the freedom given to employees, and the decision-making process.

The merger and acquisition between two culturally different companies can eventually lead to lower productivity

EXAMPLE

Daimler-Benz and Chrysler cars were fundamentally different. The first one was always known for its methodical organization and centralized decision-making, whereas Chrysler was known as a risk-taking company that encouraged creativity and flexibility. The culture differences between both companies was not diluted out by the top executives and thus failed to direct them towards increasing productivity and maximizing profit for the newly merged company.

SHAREHOLDER AND EMPLOYEE INTERESTS OVERLOOKED

One of the major mistakes committed by the parent companies is neglecting the interest of employees and shareholders during due diligence. The shareholders who are being taken over often feel hostile. Mergers and acquisitions make the employees shift their focus from productive work to issues related to conflict, layoff, and compensation. The process also puts a big question mark in the mind of employees regarding their job security.

EXAMPLES OF FIVE MAJOR MERGERS AND ACQUISITIONS THAT HAVE FAILED:

1. AOL and Time Warner   2000

2. Quaker Oats and Snapple   1993

3. BMW and Rover Cars   1994

4. Royal Bank of Scotland
and ABN AMRO   2007

5. Daimler-Benz and Chrysler   1998

Mergers and Acquisitions in the Pharmaceutical Field

Seven

Pharmaceutical Mergers and Acquisitions

Pharmaceutical mergers and acquisitions have been active since mid-1980s; as a result of these transactions, the entire industry became more concentrated among very few giant players.

The strategic considerations involved in the mergers and acquisitions varies between economies of scale, better volume of sales, better market share, and improved research and development availability and spending power.

Most of the merger deals between 1995 and 2005 were aimed at consolidation and growth orientation. The consolidation deals have always focused on profit in the long term for the acquiring company because of overlaps with the acquired company. The growth-oriented deals focus on new markets in order to push operations toward maximizing market share within these new markets.

The value of the mergers and acquisitions activities that took place from 1998 to 2000 was close to $500 billion. The top-ten global pharmaceutical players together contributed 20 percent of overall sales in 1985, and this contribution rose to 48 percent in 2005 due to the continuous merger and acquisition trend.

It is also clear that mergers were an exit strategy for the smaller pharmaceutical companies, which were not able to sustain the rapid growth of competition and spending power on research and development.

LARGEST PHARMACEUTICAL MERGERS AND ACQUISITIONS TO DATE

The largest pharmaceutical mergers and acquisitions are the following (all in USD):

- 1999: Pfizer and Warner-Lambert, $90 billion
- 2000: Glaxo Wellcome and SmithKline Beecham, $76 billion
- 2004: Sanofi and Aventis, $73 billion
- 2015: Actavis and Allergan, $70.5 billion
- 2004: Pfizer and Wyeth, $68 billion
- 2002: Pfizer and Pharmacia, $64.3 billion
- 2009: Merck and Schering-Plough, $47.1 billion
- 2014: Medtronic and Covidien, $42.3 billion
- 2015: Teva and Actavis, $40.5 billion

KEY CHALLENGES

Below are the main key challenges that usually accrue during mergers and acquisitions in the pharmaceutical field.

IDENTIFYING AND COMMUNICATING REASONS BEHIND MERGERS OR ACQUISITIONS

Employees usually see this change as a threat to their future careers due to the absence of complete information. The role of human resources is to explain to all employees at all levels the necessity of the change, the ways that they will benefit from the change, and the ways that the company will be in a better shape.

FORMING A MERGER AND ACQUISITION TEAM AND CHOOSING THE LEADER

It's important to form a merger team with a leader who will be solely focusing on the merger or acquisition process rather than being involved in running the day-to-day business. The process of any merger or acquisition involves many issues and details that need a dedicated team to look after and focus on.

FORMING THE NEW CORPORATE CULTURE

One of the major task of human resources is to make sure of the proper integration of two different cultures and to identify a new corporate culture based on clear strategy, vision, and direction.

One company may be driven by a sales mentality, while the other one may be focusing on innovation. Similarly one company may make decisions based on a top-down style, while the other company may have a participative, decision-making approach. Therefore human resources must anticipate culture challenges and take steps to integrate the two different cultures into one.

DECIDING WHO STAYS AND WHO LEAVES

One of the major challenges of any merger or acquisition is slimming down the organization chart to make it more productive, effective, and cost conscious. Therefore determining the new organization chart is one of the key challenges, as selection of staff and managers will be based on many factors, such as competence, knowledge, and experience.

COMPARISONS OF BENEFITS, COMPENSATIONS, AND UNION CONTRACTS

Another of the key challenges is how to compare benefits and compensations between the two merger companies and to come up with a new policy that can be more satisfying and beneficial to all employees.

TOP TEN PHARMACEUTICAL GIANTS

10. Gilead Sciences   **Revenue:** $24.474 billion
9. Bayer   **Revenue:** $25.47 billion
8. AstraZeneca   **Revenue:** $26.095 billion
7. GlaxoSmithKline   **Revenue:** $37.96 billion
6. Merck   **Revenue:** $42.237 billion
5. Sanofi   **Revenue:** $43.07 billion
4. Pfizer   **Revenue:** $49.605 billion
3. Roche   **Revenue:** $49.86 billion
2. Novartis   **Revenue:** $57.996 billion
1. Johnson & Johnson   **Revenue:** $74.331 billion

Eight

Glaxo Wellcome and
SmithKline Beecham Merger

January 18, 2000, marked the announcement of the United Kingdom's top pharmaceutical companies, Glaxo Wellcome and SmithKline Beecham, merging their operations together to become the world's largest drug company.

REASON BEHIND THE MERGER

Prior to the merger between the two companies in question, big players of the European drug market had been announcing their merging decisions. Zeneca, a UK firm, merged with Astra, a Swedish firm, while Hoescht and Rhone Poulnec also merged to form Aventis, based in France.

Moves like this allowed the huge cost savings needed for the ever-emerging, high costs of developing and marketing new drugs in a time when the demand for cheaper pharmaceuticals was fundamental to health services throughout the world. Moreover, the market share held by their competitors as a result of these strategic mergers bore a great threat to the companies if they did not come together.

Merck had a market share of 4.2 percent, while the expected merger of Pfizer and Warner-Lambert would have a market share of 6.3 percent, leaving Glaxo Wellcome to trail behind. However, with the combination, Glaxo SmithKline would become the world's biggest producer of prescription drugs; this would place them at the number-one position with a market share of 7 percent.

KEY FEATURES OF THE PARTNERSHIP
The partnership included these features:

- Largest research and development budget in the industry, allowing enhanced R&D capabilities
- Global sales force of forty thousand people, with seven thousand two hundred in the United States alone

- Global headquarters at GSK House, Brentford, London, officially opened in 2002 by the then prime minister, Tony Blair
- Extensive development pipeline of thirty chemical forms and nineteen vaccines
- Worldwide job losses of fifteen thousand jobs and UK job losses of five thousand jobs
- Position as the market leader in four of the largest therapeutic categories in the pharmaceutical industry

PARTNERSHIP OUTCOME

The partnership experienced the following outcomes:

- Global drugs sales of £17 billion
- Joint R&D operations with savings of £250 million
- Position as the world's largest producer of prescription drugs, with a market share of 7 percent
- Integration of SmithKline Beechum's strong consumer-oriented marketing strategies, allowing improved marketing communication within the industry and enhance sales
- Enlarged portfolio of products, allowing GSK to represent 50 percent of the global pharmaceutical market and gain a leading position in vaccines
- Operational synergies and overlap of administration, selling, manufacturing, and marketing, allowing cost savings estimated to £750 million
- Enlarged geographical presence derived from Glaxo Wellcome's presence outside of the United States

and SmithKline Beechum's strong presence within the US market, which, as one of the pharmaceutical industry's largest sales forces, increased geographical strength

Nine

Pfizer and Wyeth Acquisition

In January 2009, the board of Pfizer, the world's largest drug maker, announced an acquisition of its industry rival Wyeth for $68 billion in the largest pharmaceutical merger and acquisition transaction of the decade. Following the announcement, the stock price of Wyeth rose by 12.6 percent and of Pfizer by 1.4 percent, indicating positive market expectations for both companies. The deal was finalized after all the regulatory approvals were achieved from government authorities.

REASON BEHIND THE ACQUISITION

The combined company created one of the most diversified companies in the global health care industry. Operating through patient-centric businesses that matched the speed and agility of small, focused enterprises with the benefits of a global organization's scale and resources. Thus, the company was able to respond more quickly and effectively to meet changing health care needs. The combined company provided product offerings in numerous growing therapeutic areas, a strong product pipeline, leading scientific and manu-facturing capabilities, and a premier global footprint. Below you may find the top forces behind the acquisition.

IMPROVING THE TARGET COMPANY'S PERFORMANCE
Buying a company with the purpose of reducing costs pres-ents opportunities to improve profit margins, improve cash flow, and accelerate revenue growth. Private equity firms of-ten employ this rationale, as it tends to complement their skill sets and offers a direct line to increasing bottom-line profits.

REMOVING EXCESS CAPACITY FROM AN INDUSTRY
In mature industries, participants have often developed ex-cess capacity and thus generate more supply than demand; this does not necessarily refer just to manufacturing facilities but also refers to other resources, such as sales capacity and research and development capacity.

The difficulty with this strategy is the possibility of not having the required return on investment.

CREATING MARKET ACCESS FOR PRODUCTS
Often, smaller acquired companies don't have sufficient ac-cess to market outlets for their products because of limited resources, channels, and distribution network, which may restrict sales. Bringing an acquisition into a larger entity can quickly grow sales in a way unavailable without such a transaction.

PICKING WINNERS EARLY ON TO HELP THE BUSINESS
Making acquisitions in new, growing areas before the full potential of the area is realized, can provide a catapult for the acquired company and return large value to the buyer.

CONSOLIDATING TO IMPROVE COMPETITIVE BEHAVIOR
Deals done for the sake of removing competition tend not to succeed. In most cases, pricing behavior doesn't change, and there will be little benefit from the acquisition.

KEY FEATURES OF THE PARTNERSHIP
The partnership included these features:

- Position as leader in biologics
- Entry into the vaccine market
- Establishment of a lower and more flexible cost base
- Creation of new opportunities for established products
- Pfizer shareholder ownership of approximately 84 percent of the stock in the combined company
- Pfizer's acquisition of all outstanding Wyeth common shares, then valued at $50.19 per share
- Strong revenue diversification from stable, growing areas
- Leadership positions in key, growing therapeutic areas
- Expansion of Pfizer's presence in nonprescription pharmaceutical markets, most notably consumer health care and animal health
- Pfizer-Wyeth combined workforce reduction of 15 percent

PARTNERSHIP OUTCOME

The partnership created these outcomes:

- The company's portfolio diversified away from the intensely competitive markets.
- Pfizer's long-term exit from the cardiovascular therapy area meant that internal R&D was able to focus on six core disease areas: Alzheimer's disease, cancer, diabetes, inflammation, pain, and schizophrenia. The merger further enhanced this strategic move at the therapy-area level; Wyeth's strong presence in the disease areas of the central nervous system and immunology and inflammation allowed this.
- Pfizer retained its industry-leading position. Prior to its acquisition of Wyeth, Pfizer had been forecast to relinquish its industry-leading position to Roche (due to the patent expiration of one of their leading products, Lipitor).

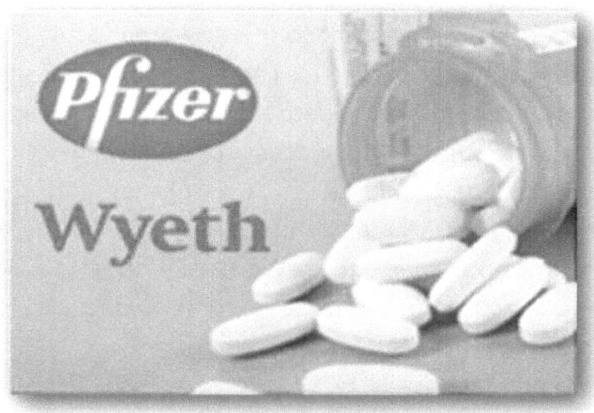

Ten

Pfizer and Warner-Lambert Acquisition

In November 1999, Pfizer and Warner-Lambert announced their intention to seal a merger worth $90 billion. The transaction was sealed in June 2000, creating the world's second-largest pharmaceutical company at that time.

REASON BEHIND THE MERGER

With this merger, Pfizer and Warner-Lambert shared a number of synergies with respect to therapy-area focus, especially in the cardiovascular products. The two companies also complemented each other in regards to their R&D pipelines.

Pfizer was particularly successful in identifying licensing opportunities for products, such as Lipitor and Celebrex, and developing products in-house, such as Viagra. On the other hand, the acquisition of Warner-Lambert provided extra strength and a number of development-stage compounds that supported Pfizer's R&D spending.

The resulting company would lead the global antihyper-tensive and antihyperlipidaemia markets. Moreover its big-gest treasure would be the cholesterol-lowering drug Lipitor, then expected to become the biggest-selling drug in the world. Lipitor, developed by Warner-Lambert and co-market-ed with Pfizer, was one of the driving forces behind the take-over battle.

KEY FEATURES OF THE PARTNERSHIP
The partnership included these features:

- Pfizer paid 2.75 of its shares for every Warner-Lambert share.
- The merging companies achieved approximately $1.6 billion in cost savings by 2002.
- The new company retained Pfizer's name and New York headquarters and was run by Pfizer's chairman, William Steere.
- The company was expected to have annual revenue of $28 billion and market capitalization exceeding $230 billion and was expected to spend $4.7 billion a year on research.
- The merged company was to hold a strong position within the CNS and anti-invective's therapy areas, with sales of over $2 billion.
- Warner-Lambert and Pfizer's merger produced a strong cardiovascular-product portfolio containing two blockbuster drugs.

- The merger strengthened Pfizer's phase-two stage in the therapy areas of endocrine and gastrointestinal cancer.
- The new company's consumer-products division—with Warner products like Listerine, Rolaids, and Sudafed—was managed from Warner-Lambert's headquarters in Morris Plains, New Jersey.
- The two companies expected to save as much as $1.6 billion in operating costs in the first two years.

PARTNERSHIP OUTCOME

The partnership experienced these outcomes:

- The resulting company led both the global antihypertensive and antihyperlipidaemia markets and became one of the leading CNS marketers.
- The acquisition of Warner-Lambert allowed Pfizer to gain product lines from Parke-Davis pharmaceuticals, such as the Listerine brand of mouthwash and the Wilkinson Sword wet-shave products.
- The combination created a fast-growing pharmaceutical company well-known in the world and paved the way for discovery of new medication that would benefit people in all corners of the world.

Eleven

Aventis and Sanofi Merger

In April 2004, Aventis, the Strasbourg, France–head-quartered pharmaceutical company, announced that it had agreed to merge with its French competitor, Sanofi-Synthelabo. This announcement came after Sanofi increased its take-over-bid price to acquire Aventis to €54.5 billion and brought to an end the three-month battle for a controlling equity stake in Aventis between Sanofi and Switzerland-based pharmaceutical company Novartis.

The merged entity, Sanofi-Aventis, emerged as the third-largest pharmaceutical company in the world, in terms of revenue, behind Pfizer and GlaxoSmithKline. This merger was a unique one because of the proactive role played by the French government in the take-over battle; the government pressured Aventis to accept the Sanofi acquisition bid.

REASON BEHIND THE MERGER

The move was expected to create the world's third-largest medicine producer behind Pfizer and GlaxoSmithKline.

France's then prime minister, Jean-Pierre Raffarin, said that "The choice of a merger between Sanofi and Aventis will allow the preservation of decision centers and jobs in France and Europe, and is in line with a strategic interest."

Sanofi wanted to buy Aventis partly to avoid becoming a target itself after a key shareholder pact between L'Oréal and Total expired in December. The cosmetics and oil companies together owned 44 percent of Sanofi.

The synergies were persuasive. Aventis had a powerful presence in the huge US market but a relatively weak inventory of new drugs, while Sanofi was the opposite with a full pipeline but a poor presence in the United States.

KEY FEATURES OF THE PARTNERSHIP

The partnership included these features:

- The company now offered investors five of its shares, plus €120 in cash for every six Aventis shares.
- The Sanofi-Aventis board of directors appointed Jürgen Dormann as vice chairman of the board.
- The merger exchange ratio was set at twenty-seven Sanofi-Aventis ordinary shares for twenty-three Aventis ordinary shares.
- The merger created a research and development portfolio of 128 products in total.
- Jean-Francois Dehecq, chairman and chief executive of Sanofi-Synthelabo, was made chairman and chief executive officer of the new entity.

- The new company had an audit committee, a remuneration committee, a scientific committee, and a strategic committee. Aventis and Sanofi had equal representation in each committee.
- Aventis's CEO Igor Landau stepped down.

PARTNERSHIP OUTCOME

The partnership experienced the following outcomes:

- On August 11, 2004, they announced a public offer for 20 percent of the capital of Aventis Pharma Limited India, which was 50.1 percent owned by Aventis's subsidiary Hoechst AG.
- On August 23, 2004, Sanofi-Aventis announced a mandatory public offer for the 1.91 percent of the capital of Hoechst AG not held by Sanofi-Aventis. Also Aventis announced its intention to acquire the shares of the outstanding shareholders of Hoechst AG through a squeeze-out transaction.
- A year after the deal, they decided to shut four out of five main headquarters, leaving just one site in Paris. Sanofi-Aventis closed down seventy local head offices around the world.
- In 2004, they reported revenue of €14,871, and in 2005, a year after the merger, the revenue was reported as €27,311.

Twelve

Actavis and Allergan Acquisition

In February 2015, it was announced that Actavis PLC Ireland acquired and took control of the whole of Allergan Inc. by way of purchasing shares in a deal worth $66 billion.

Actavis was an integrated, global, specialty-pharmaceutical company engaged in the development, manufacturing, marketing, sale, and distribution of branded originator, branded generic, biosimilar, and over-the-counter pharmaceutical products. Actavis executive offices are located in Dublin and listed on the New York Stock Exchange.

Allergan was a multispecialty health-care company with a portfolio of pharmaceutical, biological, and medical devices and over-the-counter consumer products with a focus on several medical specialists. The Allergan corporate headquarter is located in California and listed on the New York Stock Exchange.

The deal was the fourth biggest in the history of pharmaceutical mergers and acquisitions and the largest in the decade, since the $73.5 billion Sanofi acquisition of Aventis.

REASONS BEHIND THE MERGER

The combined company would be recognized for its strong commitment as the partner of choice with physicians, specialists, pharmacists, regulators and patients. The combination would be committed to creating the best customer experience, based on deeply-held relationships with customers and colleagues in approximately 100 countries around the world, with an enhanced presence across Canada, Europe, Southeast Asia, Latin America and a strong footprint in China and India.

The combined company benefited from Allergan's global brand equity, industry-leading consumer marketing capabilities and strong consumer awareness of key Allergan products in global markets, including BOTOX®, RESTASIS®, JUVEDERM®, LATISSE®, NATRELLE®. At the time of the merger, the newly formed company was expected to have approximately $5 billion in 2015 international revenue, and have the unique opportunity to drive continued growth in international markets through its enhanced portfolio of brands, generics, branded-generic and over-the-counter products.

The combined company provided a strong commitment to R&D, with an exceptional level of investment of approximately $1.7 billion (in 2015), focused on the strategic development of innovative and durable value-enhancing products within brands, generics, biologics and OTC portfolios.

KEY FEATURES OF THE PARTNERSHIP

The partnership included these features:

- Leadership in a new industry model, growth pharma, anchored by world-renowned brand franchises; a leading, global generics business; a premier pharmaceutical-development pipeline; and an experienced management team
- Double-digit accretion to non-GAAP earnings in the first twelve months and strong, free cash flow of more than $8 billion in 2016, which would enable the company to rapidly deliver the balance sheet
- Expanded international presence in approximately one hundred countries
- Strong commitment to R&D, with an investment of approximately $1.7 billion expected in 2015, and focus on the strategic development of innovative and durable value-enhancing products within brands, generics, biologics, and OTC portfolio.
- Payment of a combination of $129.22 in cash and 0.3683 Actavis shares for each share of Allergan common stock
- Sales from the manufacture of Botox, which generated nearly $2 billion in sales in 2013 for Allergan
- Brenton L. Saunders as chief executive and president
- Paul Bisaro as executive chairman of the board of the merged company
- Operations from both California, where Allergan is based, and New Jersey

- Tax rate of 15 percent compared with Allergan's previous rate of about 26 percent

PARTNERSHIP OUTCOME

The partnership experienced the following outcomes:

- Allergan became one of the largest pharmaceutical companies in the world.
- Actavis moved its headquarters to Ireland, saving it a substantial amount in tax payments.
- After the deal was completed in March 2015, Actavis then took the better-known Allergan name.

Thirteen

Merck and Schering-Plough Merger

In November 2009, Merck & Co. and Schering-Plough announced the completion of $41.1 billion merger. They continued the combined operations under the Merck name after the deal gained clearance from regulatory authorities in China and Mexico.

Under the terms of the agreement, Schering-Plough shareholders received 0.57 shares of the newly combined company and $10.50 in cash for each share of Schering-Plough. Each Merck common share automatically became a common share of the newly combined company.

REASONS BEHIND THE MERGER

The existence of a strong formula of growth and a strong complementary portfolio broadened the scope of Merck's commercial portfolio with leading franchises in key therapeutic areas. Additionally Schering-Plough products provided long-lived marketing exclusivity.

The merger enhanced Merck's R&D efforts, spending power, and pipeline. It also added high-potential early-, mid-, and late-stage candidates to provide a platform for sustainable growth.

The partnership created an expanded global presence; the new merged company was expected to dramatically accelerate Merck's international-growth efforts especially in key emerging markets.

With the two companies' substantial synergies, there was an expected annual cost saving of $3.5 billion up to and beyond 2011. The merger was to enhance the company's financial strength and create strong, free cash flow generated by the combined companies.

The merger created opportunities for leveraging the cholesterol franchise through a future combination with Zeltia.

Schering-Plough's expertise in novel biological products complemented Merck's bio ventures technology. Also Schering-Plough's therapeutic area of focus complemented those of Merck

The chief executive said that the deal would greatly bolster Merck's presence abroad, as around 70 percent of Schering-Plough's shares were made overseas, including more than $2 billion from emerging markets. The combined company was expected to draw more than 50 percent of its revenue from outside of the United States.

KEY FEATURES OF THE PARTNERSHIP
The partnership included these features:

- By agreeing to acquire Wyeth, Pfizer added biotechnology drugs, vaccines, and consumer-health products to its lineup.
- Schering-Plough brought to Merck biotech, consumer-health, and animal-health businesses, as well as an expanded presence in Brazil, China, and other emerging markets.
- Merck took on $8.5 billion in debt to help pay for the deal.
- Schering-Plough shareholders got 0.5767 share of Merck and $10.50 in cash for each share they owned.
- Merck was expected to reap huge cost savings from the Schering-Plough merger by cutting 15 percent of the combined workforce.
- Upon completion, Merck shareholders owned roughly 68 percent of the combined company, and Schering-Plough shareholders owned the rest.
- Total cost savings through the merger were expected to be about $3.5 billion.
- After the combination, no one product would account for more than 10 percent of sales.
- The deal bolstered Merck's presence in biopharmaceuticals, an area the company had targeted for growth.
- The acquisition was financed by three sources: 17 percent of the acquisition with cash, 32 percent with debt, and 51 percent with shares.

PARTNERSHIP OUTCOME

The partnership experienced the following outcomes:

- The Schering-Plough deal helped Merck to cut costs, expand globally, and build its pipeline of biotechnology-style drugs.
- The deal gave Merck full rights to the cholesterol drugs Vytorin and Zetia—which were previously in a joint venture with Schering—and rights to the anti-inflammatory blockbuster Remicade in certain countries and other products.

Mergers and
Acquisitions in the
Airline Industry

Fourteen

Mergers and Acquisitions in the Airline Industry

The global airline industry has always been characterized by slack passenger demand and soaring fuel prices. The slowdown of the global economy has encouraged major airline companies in focusing on improving profitability, controlling cost and enlarging market share (especially in markets where they already have a strong presence) instead of engaging in competition and turf wars. Mergers, joint ventures and other strategic alliances are slowly becoming the norm for airline industry participants who are focusing on cost cutting and excess capacity reduction.

A SHIFT IN FOCUS FROM MARKET SHARE TO PROFITABILITY

The global airline industry is characterized by slack passenger demand, soaring fuel prices, and a slowdown in the global economy. The industry is cyclical, and its performance is closely linked to GDP growth.

Instead of getting engaged in competition for market share, all major airlines companies are now focusing more on improving profitability, especially in markets where they already have a strong presence. Mergers, acquisitions, joint ventures, and other strategic alliances are slowly becoming the trend and the norm for the entire industry.

REASONS BEHIND MERGERS AND ACQUISITIONS

Synergy is the most important of all reasons for mergers and acquisitions. However, we can summarize the other reasons as follows.

If an airline is strong in a particular region that the aquifer isn't and if it's more cost-effective to buy or to merge with the other airlines than to embark on a multiyear process to grow and expand into that market, it will look for a partnership. For example, if an airline company is strong and has its fair share in Europe but is willing to stretch its presence and grow in the Asia market, that company might choose to merge with another airline company with a strong presence in the target market, such as with British Airways and Iberia.

If an airline is financially weak and cannot execute its growth plans without massive investments, it goes out and seeks to be acquired or to merge with another stronger airline.

If two separately strong airlines have little overlap in their markets with strengths in different areas but are willing get stronger and bigger to be able to internationally compete and gain larger market share, they will get into a merger activity.

If an airline is facing financial challenges and its stock market is devaluating, it could be a target for another stronger airline to launch a hostile take-over.

KEY EXAMPLES OF EUROPEAN AND AMERICAN AIRLINE MERGERS AND ACQUISITIONS

1. KLM merged with Air France to make Air France KLM in 2004

2. American Airlines today, is the result of the following:
Trans Caribbean Airways – M&A transaction in 1971
Air California - M&A transaction in 1987
Reno Air - M&A transaction in 1997
TWA - M&A transaction in 2001
US Airways - M&A transaction in 2013

3. Northwest Airlines today, is the result of the following:
Republic Airlines - M&A transaction in 1986
Delta Airlines - M&A transaction in 2008

4. Lufthansa today, is the result of the following:
Sun Express Airlines - M&A transaction in 1989
Air Dolomites - M&A transaction in 1999
Swiss International - M&A transaction in 2005
Austrian Airlines - M&A transaction in 2008
Brussels Airlines (45%) - M&A transaction in 2008
JetBlue - M&A transaction in 2008
German Wings - M&A transaction in 2009

5. British Airways merged with Iberia 2010

6. United Airlines today, is the result of the following:
National Air Transport - M&A transaction in 1931
Pacific Air Transport - M&A transaction in 1931
Varney Airlines - M&A transaction in 1931
Capital Airlines - M&A transaction in 1961
Pan America - M&A transaction in 1985
Continental Airlines - M&A transaction in 2012

TOP TEN AIRLINE GIANTS

10. All Nippon Airways   **Revenue:** $ 14.7 billion
9. China Eastern Airlines   **Revenue**: $ 14.9 billion
8. China Southern Airlines   **Revenue:** $ 17.7 billion
7. Southwest Airlines   **Revenue:** $20.2 billion
6. International Airlines Group **Revenue:** $ 25.3 billion
5. Air France-KLM   **Revenue:** $ 28.9 billion

4. Lufthansa Group   **Revenue:** $ 35.5 billion
3. United Continental Holdings   **Revenue:** $ 37.5 billion
2. Delta Air Lines   **Revenue**: $ 40.5 billion
1. American Airlines Group   **Revenue:** $ 40.99 billion

Fifteen

Emirates and Qantas Partnership

The relationship between Qantas and Emirates Airlines significantly altered the air travel between Australia and the world. In March 2013, a Qantas flight departed for London Heathrow, not via Singapore (its traditional hub) but via Dubai, UAE. Qantas CEO Alan Joyce spoke about the new partnership in no uncertain terms: "This is the most significant partnership the Qantas Group has ever formed with another airline, moving past the traditional alliance model to a new level."

QANTAS AND ITS CHALLENGES

The core problem was its eastbound routes to Europe. The stopover at Singapore meant that the number of destinations across Europe were limited. They also had inconvenient stopovers, usually two for the typical passenger. Hence Qantas's flights to Europe presented with lengthy journey times and limited destination access. The Qantas Singapore services were mainly in demand by people wishing to travel to Europe.

The Australia–Singapore route, however, depended heavily on passengers wishing to go only to that destination: origin–destination traffic. Moreover Singapore was lacking as a destination itself and lacked extensive partnerships with other airlines at the Singapore Airport. By linking into Emirates' vast pan-European network via Dubai, Qantas picked up an additional fleet of planes and guaranteed revenues, without having to spend a lot of money on capital equipment and route development.

KEY FEATURES OF THE PARTNERSHIP
The partnership included these features:

- A seamless global network for customers and superior platform to the alliance model, as well as complimentary products services and brands

- Full coordination on pricing and scheduling
- Eight-nine weekly flights between Australia and Dubai
- Fifty-five Australian destinations online with over five thousand flights per week
- Enhanced connectivity to New Zealand and Southeast Asia
- Reciprocal awards, lounge access, and increased redemption of opportunities

PARTNERSHIP OUTCOME
The partnership experienced the following outcomes:

- Using Dubai international airport as an operational hub allowed Qantas customers far easier access to an increased number of European destinations with a single stopover point. It also allowed for easier connection to four major continents and hundreds of other destinations.
- Qantas customers benefited from increased flights from regional centers, meaning fewer multistep flights to reach European destinations.
- Business customers experienced an increase of efficient travel across Europe, North Africa, and the Middle East, as a direct result of Qantas switching to Dubai as a hub instead of Singapore.
- Customers enjoyed increased benefits and further opportunities to acquire mileage points.
- The merger created a larger network spanning four continents and encompassing over seventy cities between Australia, Africa, the Middle East, and Europe.

- The partnership created largest network of A380 aircraft offering inflight-entertainment systems and multi dedicated airport lounges.
- Approximately two million transit passengers a year with a certain spending power were injected into the Dubai economy.

Sixteen

British Airways and Iberia Merger

International Consolidated Airlines Group, S.A., often short-ened to IAG, is a Spanish-British, multinational, airline-holding company registered in Madrid, Spain, with its operational headquarters in London, England. It was formed in January 2011 by the merger of Iberia and British Airways, the flagship carrier airlines of Spain and the United Kingdom respectively.

REASON BEHIND THE MERGER

After years of negotiations and debates, British Airways PLC, widely recognized as the largest airline in the United Kingdom, signed an agreement with the Spanish airline Iberia for a £5 billion merger of the two organizations. The merger between the two companies was driven by a number of reasons which can be summarized as follows.

The new organization was able to provide customers with much-larger, combined network, as the new merged group was able to operate approximately 419 aircrafts and fly to more than two hundred destinations with few overlapping routes.

The merger eased the pressure of the severe competition that both airlines were facing due to the growth of low-cost carriers, like Ryanair and Easy Jet, and also the strong consolidation of the large European carriers, like Air France and KLM. The merger made the new company able to compete effectively with such domestic and international carriers.

Both companies were hit badly by the recession and the sharp escalation in oil prices. Both British Airways and Iberia made their biggest-ever loss in 2009, and their figures crashed down from profit to sever losses. Through the partnership, they were able to stop their financial bleeding.

The merger allowed both companies to exploit significant cost and operational synergies; they were able to combine the organization and reduce the total man power significantly. It was estimated that the annual cost saving reached approximately $530 million a year, which seemed to be the major driving force behind the merger.

One of the most important merger factors was the achievement of greater market power and market share through the combined operations. Therefore UK customers have benefited from the improved access to Iberia's strong South American network, even as Latin American and Spanish travelers benefited from British Airways's extensive presence in Asia and Europe.

Customers of British Airways and Iberia benefited from cooperation between the frequent-flyer programs for the two airlines, the availability of common passenger terminals, code sharing, and the use of passenger lounges.

THE KEY FEATURES OF THE PARTNERSHIP

The partnership included these features:

- The new company was called International Airlines Group, but the BA and Iberia brands continued to operate as usual.
- The company headquarters was in London.
- BA shareholders retained 55 percent ownership of the company.
- In total, the new group would operate 419 aircraft, fly to more than two hundred destinations, and carry a total of sixty-two million passengers a year.
- Willie Walsh took the role of the IAG chief executive, with BA's chief financial officer, Keith Williams, as the new BA chief executive.
- Between them, the two carriers had a staff of just over fifty-seven thousand people.

PARTNERSHIP OUTCOME

- IAG's was the biggest riser on the FTSE 100 in 2013.
- Iberia began to reopen some Latin American routes and after years of heavy losses, the Spanish flag-carrier was able to return a profit for 2014.
- The merger helped Iberia to be bolder than it otherwise would have been — in particular in facing down unions and cutting costs. Salary and productivity agreements between Iberia and its pilot unions and

cabin crew unions were key to the reduction of further airline costs.

Seventeen

Lufthansa Acquisition
of Swiss Air

June 6, 2005, marked the announcement of the €310 million (equal to $409 million) acquisition of Swiss International Airlines by Lufthansa.

The Lufthansa group is a global aviation group with extensive subsidiaries and equity investments including the passenger airline group, logistics, catering and other business segments.

Passenger transport is the largest business segment in the Lufthansa group which includes;

-German wings and Euro wings
-Swiss airlines
-Austrian airline
-Equity interests in Brussels and sun express airlines.

All airlines share the common objectives of meeting customers' demands in terms of safety, quality, punctuality, reliability and professional service.

The service companies which are the leaders on the global market, strengthen the Lufthansa group by exploiting growth opportunities in the cargo segment.

Lufthansa cargo is the logistics specialist within Lufthansa group.

Lufthansa Technik is the world's leading provider of maintenance, repair and overhaul services.

The portfolio of LGS sky chefs comprises catering, in flight sales and entertainment inflight service equipment and associated logistics as well as consultancy services and operations of lounges.

Swiss Air was formed in 1931 from a merger between Balair and Ad Astra Aero. For most of its seventy-one years, Swiss Air was one of the major international airlines and known as "the flying bank," due to the financial stability of the airline.

In 1960, air traffic increased quickly and allowed many airlines high-revenue yields. Swiss Air especially profited from its excellent reputation as a quality airline and from the fact that the political neutrality of Switzerland allowed the company to fly to lucrative destinations. The central location of Switzerland in Europe helped to generate revenue via transferring passengers from its base to the world.

REASON BEHIND THE ACQUISITION

The challenges of Swissair started when the top management underestimated the difficulties of acquiring Belgian Sabina airlines and German LTU airlines despite their significant capital requirements. On the other hand, the increasing competition from low cost carriers such as Ryanair and easy-Jet forced Swiss air to lose passenger revenue. In late 1980's, Swissair tried to be a major force in European aviation through merging with stronger partners subsequently (i.e. Air France, British Airways, and Lufthansa) in order to expand beyond its Swiss home market and get access to the wider European market. All these efforts were not successful enough to be materialized.

In 1990, Swiss Air decided to grow its market share through the acquisition of smaller airlines rather than get in to an alliance agreement. Accordingly, Swiss Air decided to acquire shares from the following airlines:

- Air Europe
- Sabena Airlines
- Air Liberté
- LOT airlines
- LTU
- Turkish Airlines
- Aer Lingus
- Finnair.

In the beginning, Swiss Air was predicted to have losses between 3.2 and 4 billion Swiss francs over the following three to four years of these transactions. However, in 2000, Swiss Air started to be under severe financial pressure because of the daily losses of Sabena and LTU and was unable to make payment to creditors on its large debts. With the refusal of the UBS bank to extend its line of credit, the entire Swiss

air fleet was abruptly grounded, and the entire company was at risk of bankruptcy.

The collapse of Swiss Air was the largest business
failure in Switzerland and cost the taxpayers approximately $1.6 billion, which resulted in thousands of job
losses and severely dented national pride. After this
situation, Swiss Air was a target for larger airline companies with stronger financial capabilities.

In 2005, the Swiss government, the biggest shareholder of
Swiss Air, announced the support of the buyout to Lufthansa.

KEY FEATURES OF THE PARTNERSHIP

The partnership included these features:

- Lufthansa's board and major shareholders approved
  the deal worth up to $409 million.
- Lufthansa offered approximately 14 percent of Swiss
  Air shares owned by small investors an amount of €45

million, while the larger shareholders—including the government, Novartis, Nestlé, and UBS and Credit-Suisse—received an amount of €265 million.

- Zurich airport remained the official hub for all new Swiss flights, and the entire management remained independent in Switzerland.

PARTNERSHIP OUTCOME

The partnership experienced the following outcomes:

- Swiss Air and Lufthansa have code-share arrangements with other carriers on flights between Australia and Bangkok, Australia and Frankfurt, and Australia and Singapore. On each of these routes, the merged entity had a market share of between 1 and 10 percent post acquisition, and there are several other large international carriers—including Qantas Airways, Singapore Airlines, and Thai Airways flying these routes.
- Lufthansa initially bought an 11 percent stake in Swiss in March 2005, and the company increased this share to 49 percent in 2006, once regulatory approval was granted.
- Lufthansa's Swiss shares are held by a separate company, Air Trust, on behalf of the German airline.
- Swiss achieved a SFr263 million ($211 million) net consolidated profit in 2006, its first full year in the black.

Eighteen

Air France and KLM Merger

In late 2003, KLM and Air France announced a merger deal that formed the world's largest carrier in terms of revenue generation. In February 2004, the merger deal was approved by the European commission, whereby Air France customers gained forty new routes while KLM gained an additional ninety routes.

REASON BEHIND THE MERGER

First, consolidation was necessary, particularly in Europe. It was needed to create pan-European leaders to match the size of the huge single market. Second, for the sake of economic efficiency, they had to have a common bottom line. Third, there was the tremendous asset of the combined development potential of Schiphol Airport and Paris Charles de Gaulle.

They were two efficient airlines. KLM was reaping the benefits of a radical recovery plan, and Air France was consistently posting profits; but they were at risk. They were at risk because they were middleweight champions in a heavy-weight contest. In an increasingly global industry, they needed to gain critical size.

The consensus view is that world air transport will ultimately be organized around three major alliances: Star, SkyTeam, and Oneworld. They were already acting as catalysts in the consolidation process. Therefore Air France and KLM had to belong to an alliance, but this alone was not enough. They also needed to make themselves heard and to become a stronger entity. In the long term, Air France would not have been able to do this alone. Air France–KLM guarantees that a European carrier will play a leading role in SkyTeam.

This common ambition that Air France and KLM share did not come from a desire to dominate. It came from a legitimate wish to ensure profitability for both airlines and to play a global role in the air-transport industry.

KEY FEATURES OF THE PARTNERSHIP

It was estimated that the new potential synergy would result in an improvement of €385 million to €495 million, where 60 percent was generated from cost saving and 40 percent came from incremental revenue.

Other key features included the following:

- Cost reduction, distribution, station handling, and catering
- Harmonization of sales polices
- The gradual grouping of sales and operations teams as needed
- Sharing of airport lounges
- Code sharing and coordinated flight schedules. This ensured that both companies' passengers got more destinations, especially as Air France had a stronger presence and network in Southern Europe, while KLM was particularly strong in Northern Europe.

PARTNERSHIP OUTCOME

The partnership experienced the following outcomes:

- Net income from the first financial year after the merger was €3.2 billion, which rose from 2.3 percent in 2003 to 6.7 percent in 2007.
- Air France and KLM carry more than seventy-seven million passengers per year. They operate 573 aircrafts, enabling them to fly to 243 destinations in 103 countries. Members of the joint Air France–KLM

frequent-flyer program, Flying Blue, earn miles and claim rewards on both airlines' routes.

- Both airlines run their own operations from their respective hubs: Paris Charles de Gaulle and Amsterdam's Schiphol.
- The merger created a combined workforce of some one hundred thousand employees.
- They have increased their bargaining power. For example, take aircraft purchasing: KLM's medium-haul fleet consisted of Boeing aircraft, and Air France's medium-haul fleet of Airbus aircraft. The merger created more leverage when negotiating to buy new aircrafts from the two aircraft manufacturers.
- They reduced their operating costs at outstations by integrating their international operations in each country. This was done country by country, taking into account the specificities of each region and the relative strengths of both airlines.
- They introduced the concept of combinable fares, which enables customers to fly with one carrier on the outbound flight and the other carrier on the return flight at the best possible price.
- They now have only one frequent-flyer program, Flying Blue, which has become the most powerful loyalty program in Europe with over ten million members.
- They have a single management and corporate-contract system for large accounts, and the sales representatives of both airlines make their sales calls together.

Nineteen

Etihad Airways and Air Berlin Partnership

In December 2011 after long negotiations, Etihad Airways came to an agreement to increase its share in Air Berlin, the second German airline after Lufthansa, to reach an almost 30 percent stake, making Etihad Airways Air Berlin's biggest shareholder.

As part of this strategic partnership, Air Berlin operated daily nonstop flights from Berlin, Düsseldorf, Frankfurt, and Stuttgart to Abu Dhabi, making Abu Dhabi a hub gateway to the Arab world, Asia, Africa, and Australia. The partnership supported the combined route network for the whole Etihad Group to reach a total of 350 destinations worldwide. In addition to this, frequent flyers could also collect and redeem awards miles on all Etihad Airways partner flights.

Etihad Airways was established by Royal (Amiri) Decree in July 2003. Etihad Airways commenced operations in November 2003 as a flag carrier and the second-largest airline of the UAE (after Emirates). Its head office is located in

Khalifa City, Abu Dhabi. The airline operates over 1,000 flights per week to over 120 passenger and cargo destinations in the Middle East, Africa, Europe, Asia, Australia and the Americas.

In addition to passenger transportation, Etihad also operates Etihad Holidays and Etihad Cargo. In 2015 Etihad established its own airline alliance, Etihad Airways Partners, which includes Alitalia, Jet Airways, Air Berlin, Niki, Air Serbia, Air Seychelles and Etihad Regional.

Air Berlin PLC & Co Luftverkehrs KG (branded as airberlin) is Germany's second largest airline, after Lufthansa, and Europe's seventh largest airline in terms of air passengers. Air Berlin PLC & Co. Luftverkehrs KG is the legal parent company of the airberlin group and was founded in England and Wales as a public limited company in 2005. It retains hubs at Berlin Tegel Airport, Düsseldorf Airport and operates a route network that includes a total of 17 German cities, some European metropolitan and a few leisure destinations in Southern Europe and North Africa, as well as intercontinental services to destinations in the Caribbean and the Americas.

Air Berlin is a member of the Oneworld alliance, and owns the subsidiary Belair (in Switzerland) while the sale of its 49% stake NIKI (Austrian subsidiary) to Etihad Airways was announced in December 2016.

REASON BEHIND THE PARTNERSHIP

The key attraction for Etihad Airways was Germany, Europe's largest outbound market. As Air Berlin was the number-one carrier in Berlin and Düsseldorf, it could provide Etihad

Airways with additional getaways to the German market beyond Etihad's already established Frankfurt and Munich services.

The integration of the frequent-flyer program enabled both Etihad Airways and Air Berlin customers to enjoy extended benefits and rewards. Another attraction was mutual fleet procurement, usage, maintenance, and repair, as well as general purchases of aircrafts. Finally more than thirty-six new destinations were expanded due to the code-share agreement

KEY FEATURES OF THE PARTNERSHIP
The partnership included these features:

- On the routes between Europe and Abu Dhabi, Etihad Airways customers were able to fly between Amsterdam and Abu Dhabi, five times per week; these flights were operated by KLM.
- This code-share agreement offered five destinations each to Air France and KLM's passengers on the Asian and Australian market and ten European destinations to Etihad's passengers on Air France and KLM.
- KLM shared code with Air Berlin on three destinations beyond Berlin: Krakow (Poland), Gdansk (Poland), and Kaliningrad (Russia).
- Air Berlin shared code on Berlin to Amsterdam routes, as well as on Amsterdam flights to Edinburgh (UK), Glasgow (UK), and Manchester (UK).

PARTNERSHIP OUTCOME

The partnership experienced the following outcomes:

- Other than operational benefits (expansion of its reach to the East and South; advantages in efficiency), Air Berlin was able to improve its economic stance. The extent of the collaboration between Air Berlin and Etihad Airways included flight schedules, procurement, maintenance, ground handling, and training.
- In 2014, the merged group had more than six hundred thousand passengers.
- The partnership created 213 destinations in places such as India, Australia, and South Korea; flights to eighty-one different countries; and eighty-seven code-share routes.

Mergers and Acquisitions in the Hospitality Industry

Twenty

Mergers and Acquisitions in the Hospitality Industry

Hospitality is one of the world largest industries. According to the World Tourism Organization (2015 Tourism Highlights Report), the industry contribution to the economy has reached 9.5 percent of the global GDP, with a total of 11 percent of total employment (estimated over 250 million people). This is five times more than automotive manufacturing, five times more than the global chemical industry, four times more than the global mining industry, and 15 percent more than the global financial-services industry.

Major challenges facing the global hospitality industry can be summarized in the following points.

CHANGING LABOR CONDITIONS

The hospitality industry faces labor and human-resource challenges, including shrinking labor forces, slowing population-growth rates, and increasing costs of health care and related benefits. The growth in unions and interest among employees in unions has increasingly posed challenges to hospitality-related operations.

ESCALATING OPERATING COSTS

Operating expenses have rapidly increased at a greater rate than income and thus have potential to erode the bottom line. Operating costs include energy and power, escalating insurance premiums, labor costs, labor shortages, and finally the continuous change in brand standards by the operators through raising the bar via increased services and amenities in an attempt to gain a competitive edge in the marketplace.

ESCALATING RENOVATION AND CONSTRUCTION COSTS

Increases in construction and renovation costs are resulting in escalating capital-investment exposure for many existing hotels and increased capital requirements for new construction.

For the existing hotels, many branded companies are increasingly demanding improvements and upgrades in the physical conditions of the hotels and more adherence to brand standards in order to remain competitive.

For new construction, higher costs for construction mitigate new development. There are several factors that impact the financial feasibility of new construction, and they include increased prices for building materials, higher energy costs, and rising interest costs. As a result, the cost of building hotels is rapidly increasing at a pace greater than the anticipated increases in revenue.

INCREASED CUSTOMER EXPECTATIONS
Anticipating and satisfying increased customer needs and expectations continues to remain a significant priority. Customers are increasingly sophisticated in the use of technology. As a result, operations are continually investing and regularly updating their marketing approach to meet customers' expectations and to have an edge on other operators in order to gain larger market share.

ACCELERATING CHANGE AND THE MERGING OF TECHNOLOGIES
Systems interfaces in hotels are rapidly shifting to Internet-based technology, which allows easier and more flexible integration. Hotel operators are continuously investing in and taking full advantages of this technology in order to streamline their operations. The more updates and improvements made in hotel technology, the more investment carried out by operators to continuously be up-to-date and secure their edge among other operators. As a result, costs are continually increasing as the technology develops.

THE RAPID INCREASE OF MERGERS AND CONSOLIDATIONS OF HOTEL BRANDS
Major company brands are creating specific brand niches to address micromarkets, while at the same time, they are making it more difficult for the customer to truly understand the differences in brands. What makes sense to the hotel developer or the brand becomes confusing to the customer and thus impacts both consumer pricing and commoditizing hotel products.

Public hotel companies in search of shareholder value are poised to create conditions for additional consolidation, not unlike the online world, where 80 percent of online hotel inventory is managed by only a few companies.

REASONS BEHIND INDUSTRY CONSOLIDATIONS AND MERGERS

Industry consolidations and mergers occur for the following reasons:

- Geographic and business diversifications, expansion of product portfolios, and rationalization through corporate restructuring
- Strategic leverage and economies of scale
- New market segments through different brands and concepts to gain access to larger loyalty databases
- More effective response to the challenges associated with the position of online travel agencies (OTA) as key distribution channels for hotels and the impact they have on the bottom line
- Presence in an attractive and potential destination, which can lead to an increase in the global market share

TOP TEN HOSPITALITY COMPANIES

10. Carlson Rezidor Hotel Group   **Rooms:** 172,234
9. Homeinns Hotel Group   **Rooms:** 303,768
8. Best Western Hotels and Resorts   **Rooms:** 311,608
7. Accor Hotels   **Rooms:** 500,366
6. Choice Hotels International   **Rooms:** 504,357
5. Jinjiang International/
Plateno Hotels Group   **Rooms**: 640,000
4. Wyndham Hotel Group   **Rooms:** 671,900
3. InterContinental Hotels Group   **Rooms:** 726,876
2. Hilton Worldwide Holdings   **Rooms:** 737,922
1. Marriott International/
Starwood Hotels and Resorts Worldwide   **Rooms**: 1,071,096

Twenty-One

Accor Acquisition of Fairmont Raffles Hotels International

July 12, 2016, marked the $2.7 billion purchase of Toronto-based, luxury-hotel chain Fairmont Raffles Hotels International (FRHI) by AccorHotels—the French chain that manages Sofitel, Pullman, Ibis, Mercure, and Novotel—to become the sixth-largest hotel chain in terms of room availability.

REASONS BEHIND THE ACCOR ACQUISITION

AccorHotels's presence in the North American continent, including the United States, was almost nonexistent after the company disposed of its brands Motel 6 and Studio 6 in May 2012.

With this acquisition, Accor's board included Prince Alwaleed and the Qatar Investment Authority, which belongs to the Emir of Qatar. This gave Accor huge global-development opportunities to take over more medium-sized hotel groups. The addition of Fairmont, Raffles, and Swissôtel gave

AccorHotels a luxury presence, which was expected to give AccorHotels an instant boost at the high end of the market.

KEY FEATURES OF THE PARTNERSHIP

The partnership included these features:

- Previous to the merger, FRHI's owners were the Qatar Investment Authority, Kingdom Holding (owned by the Saudi Arabia's Prince Al Waleed), and the Oxford Properties Group, Canada.
- After the merger, the Qatar investment authority and Kingdom Holding became the major shareholders with 10.5 percent and 5.8 percent of the share capital respectively, a total of 16.3 percent of available shares.
- Accor Hotels issues 46.7 million new Accor shares and a payment of $840 million (€768 million).

PARTNERSHIP OUTCOME

The partnership experienced these outcomes:

- The acquisition made Accor the world's market leader within the luxury hotel sector, as Accor had more than three thousand seven hundred hotels around the world and FRHI had 155 hotels, totaling 3,855 hotels.
- For FRHI, it meant a new stage of growth, since 75 percent of its customers were Americans. Under the umbrella of Accor, FRHI had greater potential of stretching its presence to Europe.
- The luxury hotel sector was an additional strength for Accor in a market segment in which the French had participated just marginally.
- The acquisition increased their market share in the sector of luxury hotels with the three newly added brands; approximately 35 percent of the revenue was to be generated from this sector.
- The partnership improved the presence of Accor in the North American market; one of its main drawbacks was its lack of presence in this particular area.
- The combined loyalty program managed to collect approximately three million high-end members and to drive their traffic through Europe, where the Accor brand was well established. This created greater overall exposure.
- Accor became the sixth-largest hotel chain in the world in terms of number of rooms available. This created many more opportunities for growth.

- Through the consolidation's synergies and cost saving, they expected to save close to $65 million in the years to come.
- The merger increased negotiating power with the global online-reservation system, thereby making the company able to reduce commission payments significantly.

Twenty-Two

IHG Group Acquisition of Kimpton Hotel and Restaurant Group

In January 2015, InterContinental Hotels Group (IHG) acquired Kimpton Hotel and Restaurant Group by for a cash sum of $430 million.

Kimpton Hotel and Restaurant Group was the world's largest independent boutique hotel chain and food and beverage operator; it managed sixty-two hotels in United States as well as seventy-one sophisticated restaurants and bars. Established in 1981, it had a strong presence across twenty-eight cities in the United States, offering a wide range of high-end guest needs including mixing business with pleasure, short-break-from experiences, romantic getaways, and well-being at an upscale price point.

Kimpton hotels and restaurants secured a wealth of industry awards and accolades including the following:

- *Fortune* magazine's one hundred best companies to work for

- The number-one company for guest satisfaction for North American upper upscale hotel brands in 2013 and 2014
- The best performing company in overall customer satisfaction by the Market Matrix Hospitality Index
- Best hotel bars by food and wine in 2014 by Trip Advisor

IHG Group was a holding company incorporated in Great Britain. The IHG Group franchised, leased, managed, and owned over four thousand seven hundred hotels and six hundred ninety-seven thousand guest rooms in nearly one hundred countries and had almost one thousand two hundred hotels in the development pipeline.

IHG had a strong portfolio of nine hotel brands including InterContinental Hotels and Resorts, Hotel Indigo, Crowne Plaza Hotels and Resorts, Holiday Inn hotels and resorts, Holiday Inn Express Suites, Candlewood Suites, Even hotels, and Hualuxe Hotels and Resorts. These brands cover all types of customers' needs and budgets around the globe.

REASON BEHIND THE MERGER

Adding Kimpton to IHG's portfolio, alongside the Indigo and Even hotel brands, created a leading boutique and lifestyle hotel business with over two hundred hotels across nineteen countries with a strong possibility to expand the reputation to the European market.

Boutique hotels segment had been the fastest growing in the hospitality industry with demand, supply, and RevPAR growth for boutique hotels significantly outperforming the overall industry.

IHG Group capitalized on its powerful, global owner network and specialist capabilities in order to:

a) build preferred brands to enhance Kimpton's global growth in Asia and Europe

b) benefit from Kimpton's strong track record in operational excellence and food and beverage reputation and add it to its current brand portfolio.

The acquisition of Kimpton enlarged the IHG Group's loyalty-program customer base, which had reached globally to ninety-two million members, and stretched their presence in the United States, where Kimpton was based.

KEY FEATURES OF THE PARTNERSHIP

The partnership included these key features:

- Clear market leadership for IHG in the boutique segment, the fastest growing segment in the industry
- Significant opportunities for IHG to accelerate the growth of the Kimpton brand within the United States and to launch it globally

- Compelling financial rationale, with Kimpton EBITDA expected to double by the end of 2017
- Earnings enhancement in the first full year and returns above IHG's cost of capital by year three

PARTNERSHIP OUTCOME

Outcomes of the partnership include the following:

- For US tax purposes, the transaction constituted an asset sale for both the vendor and purchaser, and IHG was entitled to amortize the assets acquired.
- The relief associated with this amortization was expected to reduce future taxes by approximately $160 million.

Twenty-Three

Marriott Acquisition of Starwood

In November 2015, Marriott International announced the acquisition of its rival Starwood, the owner of a series of such brands as Sheraton, W Hotels, and St Regis Hotels and Resorts. The deal, which cost $12.2 billion, created the world's largest hotel chain. The new company owned five thousand five hundred properties and more than 1.1 million rooms scattered around the globe.

The stock and cash deal added 50 percent more rooms in the Marriott portfolio and gave it more unique, designed-focused hotels that appeal to younger travelers. The merger was expected to deliver annual cost savings of at least $200 million in the second full year.

REASON BEHIND THE ACQUISITION

In total, the merger put thirty hotel brands under the Marriott umbrella and thus created the largest hotel chain in the world. This eclipsed Hilton World wide's seven hundred seventy-three thousand rooms and InterContinental's seven hundred sixty-six thousand rooms. It gave Marriott the ability to offer many more choices, locations, and interests and more spending power, and the thirty different brands met with all differences in customer budgets and spending power.

The combination of two of the most powerful loyalty programs ensured increased, effective coverage to millions of loyal customers of both brands. The purchase also gave Marriott more leverage with the corporate-travel department, which often looks for one giant chain to house all employees.

The purchase gave Marriott more over the OTA suppliers that sell the rooms on behalf of the hotel when negotiating the commission scheme. The entire hotel industry is always trying to get travelers to book directly with the hotel instead of travel agencies in order to avoid paying this commission.

KEY FEATURES OF THE PARTNERSHIP

The partnership included these features:

- Marriott matched member status across Marriott Rewards—including the Ritz-Carlton Rewards—and Starwood Preferred Guest (SPG), enabling members to transfer points between the programs for travel and exclusive experiences when they linked their accounts.
- Bruce Duncan, Eric Hippeau, and Aylwin Lewi were appointed to the Marriott board.
- The new company operated or franchised more than five thousand seven hundred properties and 1.1 million rooms.
- The merger created a company with thirty leading brands from the moderate to luxury tiers in over 110 countries.
- Marriott's distribution more than doubled in Asia and the Middle East and Africa combined.
- One-time transaction costs for the merger were expected to total approximately $140 million.
- Marriott's board of directors increased from eleven to fourteen members.
- Arne Sorenson remained president and chief executive officer of Marriott International, and Marriott's headquarters continued to be located in Bethesda, Maryland.
- Starwood's shareholders received twenty-one dollars in cash and 0.80 shares of Marriott International, Inc.

PARTNERSHIP OUTCOME

The partnership experienced these outcomes:

- The acquisition closed on September 23, 2016. At quarter-end, the company had nearly 1.6 million rooms open or in the development pipeline.
- During the three months ending in September 30, 2016, Marriott and Starwood together added more than seventeen thousand six hundred rooms, including approximately one thousand six hundred rooms converted from competitor brands and nearly eight thousand six hundred rooms in international markets.
- On a pro-forma basis reflecting the performance for both companies for the three months ending September 30, 2016, North American, comparable, system-wide, constant-dollar RevPAR rose 2.6 percent, while worldwide, comparable, system-wide, constant-dollar RevPAR rose 2.2 percent.
- Third-quarter, adjusted net income totaled $235 million, a 12 percent increase over the prior year's results.

Mergers and Acquisitions in the Oil Sector

Twenty-Four

Mergers and Acquisitions in the Oil Sector

Since the collapse of oil prices dropped from $110 per barrel to below forty dollars, the industry has come to realize that lower and increased price volatility are the new norms. The dramatic shift has affected the whole sector from the independent private companies and national oil companies to oil-field service companies and equipment manufacturers. With this dramatic change, the priority was to respond rapidly with significant cost and CapEx (capital expenditure) reductions to secure cash flow.

The longer the low prices and high-cost structure continued, the more the new reality was taking over, which was the necessity to go through merger or acquisition activities to reduce costs and enlarge market share. Small oil services companies became targets of bigger oil companies. From this point on, the mergers and acquisitions trend started.

KEY EXAMPLES OF THE WORLD'S LARGEST MERGERS AND ACQUISITIONS IN THE OIL INDUSTRY

1. Sinopec, owned by the Chinese government (Total assets $226.6 billion; annual revenue $455.06 billion).

Sinopec is the result of the following acquisitions;

2001 New Star Petroleum Company

2006 Hainan Petrochemical Company

2006 Chengli Petroleum Company

2009 Addax Petroleum Corp.

2011 Daylight Energy

2. China National Petroleum, owned by the Chinese government (Total assets $481.07 billion; annual revenue $432 billion).

China National Petroleum is the result of the following acquisition;

2005 Petro Kazakhstan.

3 Royal Dutch Shell (Total assets $353.16 billion; annual revenue$ 422.11 billion).

Royal Dutch Shell is the result of the following acquisitions;

1919 Mexican Eagle Petroleum

1979 Solahart

1985 Shell Oil

2002 Enterprise Energy Ireland

2006 Shell Canada

2010 East Resources

2015 BG Group

4 Exxon Mobil (Total assets $349.49 billion; annual revenue $394.11 billion).
Exxon Mobil is the result of the following acquisitions;
1879 Vacuum Oil Company
1959 Humble Oil
1999 Mobil Corp.
2010 XTO Energy

5 Saudi Aramco, owned by the Saudi government (Total assets $30 trillion; annual revenue $378 billion).
Saudi Aramco is the result of the following acquisition;
1980 Aramco

6 BP (Total assets $284.3 billion; annual revenue $358 billion).
BP is the result of the following acquisitions;
1978 Standard Oil of Ohio
1998 Amoco Oil
2000 Arco
2000 Burma Castro

7 Total SA (Total asset $229.7 billion; annual revenue $260 billion).
Total SA is the result of the following acquisitions;
1980 Vickers Petroleum
1999 Pertofina
2000 Elf Aquitaine
2011 Sun Power

8 Kuwait Petroleum Corp. (Total assets unknown; annual revenue $251.9 billion).

9 Chevron Corporation (Total assets $266.02 billion; Annual revenue $192.3 billion)
Chevron Corporation is the result of the following acquisitions;
1984 Gulf Oil
2000 Texaco
2005 Unocal Corporation

10 Lukoil (Total assets $111.35 billion; annual revenue $114.17 billion)
Lukoil is the result of the following acquisitions;
2000 Getty Oil
2004 Scholtzmeyer Bros
2008 Akpet

TOP TEN OIL COMPANIES

10. OJSC Lukoil **Revenue:** $144.17 billion
9. Total SA **Revenue:** $212 billion
8. BP **Revenue:** $222.8 billion
7. Kuwait Petroleum Corporation **Revenue:** $251.94 billion
6. Royal Dutch Shell **Revenue:** $265 billion
5. Exxon Mobil **Revenue:** $268.9 billion
4. Petro China **Revenue:** $367.982 billion
3. China National Petroleum
Corporation **Revenue**: $428.62 billion
2. Sinopec Re**venue:** $455.499 billion
1. Saudi Aramco **Revenue:** $478.00 billion

Twenty-Five

Exxon and Mobil Merger

November 30, 1999, marked the announcement of the
$73.7 billion merger between Exxon, a New Jersey
oil company, and Mobil, a New York oil company, to form
ExxonMobil, which became the largest oil company as well as
the third-largest corporation in the world.

REASON BEHIND THE MERGER
One of the major catalysts behind the recent mergers in the
petrochemical industry was the ongoing, falling price of crude
oil—a result of oversupply in the market and slow-moving demand, resulting in particular from the deepening economic
slump in Asia and the contraction of world growth in 1997. In
1996, the price of a barrel of crude oil dropped to as low as
$9.87 in London and $10.85 in the United States—a decline in
price of almost 50 percent.

Oil-market analysts stated that oil prices, when adjusted for inflation, were at their lowest level since the Great
Depression. Asia's economic slump, Iraq's fragmentary return

to oil markets, increased supplies from West Africa, and increased natural-gas use knocked the bottom out of the world market. This compressed profit margins despite technology-driven reductions in production costs. Moreover, during that period, the price of oil was not expected to rise in the near future. The major oil companies sought to consolidate their operations and develop economies of scale to produce huge savings, increase market share, combine resources for costly oil exploration, and increase profitability.

KEY FEATURES OF THE PARTNERSHIP
The partnership included these features:

- Mobil's shareholders received 1.32 of Exxon's shares for each Mobil share.

- Lee Raymond, the head of Exxon, remained the chairman and chief executive of the new company.
- Lucio Noto, Mobil chief executive, became vice chairman.
- The workforce was slashed by 7 percent, equivalent to fourteen thousand employees.
- Exxon shareholders owned 70 percent of the new company.
- Mobil shareholders owned 30 percent of the merged group.
- The merger brought $2.8 billion in savings.
- The new company operated forty-eight thousand service stations.
- Exxon Mobil's worldwide downstream headquarters were in Fairfax, Virginia.

PARTNERSHIP OUTCOME

The partnership experienced these outcomes:

- Shares rose by 85 percent.
- ExxonMobil generated one of America's biggest annual profits in corporate history which happened in 2008 with posted sales of $459.58 billion and net income of $45.22 billion.
- Assets rose to $233.32 billion, from $96.06 billion for Exxon.
- In 1997, Exxon had reserves of 42.13 billion cubic feet of natural gas and 6.79 billion barrels of oil. In 2009, it had total reserves of 22.99 billion barrels of

oil equivalent, including 8.9 billion barrels of oil and sixty-eight billion cubic feet of natural gas.

- The company gained a stronger position in the areas of the world with the highest potential for future oil and gas discoveries.
- The merger allowed for a more strategic position to invest in programs involving large expenses with high risks and returns.
- Operating synergies between the two companies were successfully achieved by omitting duplicate facilities and excess capacity.
- Combined general and administrative costs were significantly reduced.
- The merger enabled the new company to dominate larger operations around the globe, from Africa to the Far East and from Eastern Canada to South America.

EXXON/MOBIL FINANCIAL RELATIONS

	EXXON	MOBIL
MARKET VALUE (BILLION $)	175	58.7
BOOK VALUE (BILLION $)	437	19

Twenty-Six

British Petroleum and Amoco Oil Merger

In August 1998, it was announced that British Petroleum PLC (BP) was acquiring the American oil giant Amoco for an amount of $48.2 billion in stock. This deal was the largest oil-industry merger ever. The deal would also be the largest take-over of an American company by a foreign concern.

When the merger was approved by the regulators and shareholders of both companies, BP Amoco was the world's third-largest multinational oil company in terms of net income, after Exxon Corporation and the Royal Dutch Shell group of companies.

The new merger deal allowed both companies to benefit, since the main strength of British Petroleum was searching and finding oil reserves but, on the other hand, the company was weak in the business of refining oil into products and chemicals and the distribution process to consumers. The strengths of Amoco oil were those that British Petroleum were lacking: natural gas reserves and petrochemicals.

REASON BEHIND THE MERGER

This merger brought both assets of British Petroleum into a larger, far more comprehensive structure and made the new merged company a true giant with an enhanced and powerful structure supporting each other's weaknesses.

The merger allowed the new company to consolidate spending power on oil and gas explorations, these explorations would exceed other giant competitors like Exxon Corporation and Royal Dutch Shell.

Also the merger created the opportunity for the new company to be more present in and able to compete in new regions like Russia, China, and Latin America, where competition in these regions was becoming severe and aggressive, as companies were focusing on new sources of generating revenues.

It was expected that the new merger could set off a wave of consolidations in oil companies unlike that seen in financial services and telecommunications industries, since the major players in the oil industry relied most on joint ventures rather than comprehensive acquisitions to increase profitability.

In such a climate of oil-price fluctuations, the best investment opportunities would go increasingly to companies with the size and financial strength to take on those large-scale projects that offer truly distinctive returns. The merger put the new company in that league.

The combined company had 9.2 billion barrels of crude oil in reserve, and the merged company would also be the largest natural-gas producer in North America. On the other hand, BP became the largest company in the United Kingdom, supplanting the pharmaceutical manufacturer Glaxo Wellcome.

KEY FEATURES OF THE PARTNERSHIP
The partnership included these key features:

- BP held a 60 percent equity interest, and Amoco held 40 percent.
- The merger created operational synergies and cost savings of at least $2 billion.
- The new combined company had leadership positions in oil in Alaska, the Gulf of Mexico, the North Sea, and the Caspian Sea.
- It held reserves of about 14.8 billion BOE (barrel of oil equivalent) and produced about 3 million BOE.
- The new company had a world-class series of chemical businesses.
- Amoco shareholders received 3.97 BP ordinary shares for each Amoco share held at the day of the merger finalization.
- The Amoco chairman and CEO, Laurence Fuller, and the BP chairman, Peter Sutherland, became cochairmen of the board of BP Amoco.
- BP CEO John Browne became chief executive.
- The partnership reduced costs by eliminating areas of overlap between the two organizations—most notably in the reduction of approximately ten thousand jobs.

PARTNERSHIP OUTCOME
The partnership experienced the following outcomes:

- The merger not only added substantially to BP's oil operations, but more importantly it also gave the company a leadership position in natural gas. With demand for gas expected to grow much faster than demand for oil in the coming years, it was critical for BP to move in that direction.

- In the long term, the pooling of BP and Amoco's assets and revenues allowed the company to finance more development and take on larger projects.
- In 2000, the company shed "Amoco" from its name, becoming simply "BP PLC." The well-known Amoco name and logo were replaced with a new BP logo and color scheme—a green-and-yellow sunburst. Industry analysts speculated that the changes were intended to help the company move away from its longstanding identity as an oil company and reposition itself as an energy company, with operations in oil, natural gas, and solar power.
- In 2000, the company made $12 billion in pretax profits—a record for a UK company.

Mergers and Acquisitions in the Retail & Services Field

Twenty-Seven

Mergers and Acquisitions in the Retail & Services Field

In the retail field, mergers and acquisitions activities are more common and active than in any other field. In mature markets, mergers and acquisitions can often be the easier way of obtaining growth rather than attempting to have an edge on competitors and gain market share. In developing markets, mergers and acquisitions provide a way of obtaining a launch pad from which future growth can be obtained, and developing markets that already exist provide local management expertise as part of the launch.

The trend of mergers and acquisitions is expected to continue in mature markets due to the strong cash positions of leading consumer-goods companies. In developing markets, acquisitions of many small players may emerge as an important strategy.

CHALLENGES FACING ACQUISITIONS IN THE RETAIL FIELD

One of the major challenges facing companies is the lack of mergers and acquisition experience within the leadership team, as they should possess knowledge about the integration process, culture, strength, and weaknesses of the entire operation.

Another major challenge is the difference in the companies' values, beliefs, work style, and behavior and the means of ensuring a proper integration between the two cultures. The ability to combine the two different cultures of the merged companies and direct them towards achieving a new company strategy and goals based on achieving profit.

The involvement of operating teams is another challenge. In some companies, the CEO or the corporate-development department conclude the merger or the acquisition; then they hand it over to the operating executives to integrate and operate, which dramatically increases the integration complexity and the risk of failure. Other companies involve their operating executives and expose them to all details of the integration, which automatically decreases the risk of failure and improves the productivity and future outcome.

The final challenge is clarity. When acquiring a retail business, one of the major factors that can harm a deal or make the deal a successful is the availability of complete and correct data and information. If information or data are not completely accurate, this will definitely lead to a great loss after the deal has been concluded, and it will take time to diagnose the reasons for the losses and time to fix them. The acquirer will thus find the return on investment to have vanished.

TOP TEN RETAIL GIANTS

10. Target Corporation   **Revenue:** $72.6 billion
9. The Home Depot, Inc.   **Revenue**: $83.2 billion
8. Metro Group   **Revenue:** $85.5 billion
7. Amazon.com   **Revenue:** $89 billion
6. Carrefour SA   **Revenue:** $99.1 billion
5. Tesco PLC   **Revenue:** $101.3 billion
4. Walgreens Boots Alliance, Inc.   **Revenue:** $103.4 billion
3. Kroger Company   **Revenue:** $108.5 billion
2. Costco Wholesale Corporation   **Revenue**: $112.6 billion
1. Wal-Mart Stores, Inc.   **Revenue:** $485.7 billion

Twenty-Eight

Facebook Acquisition of WhatsApp

February 2014 marked the announcement of Facebook's biggest acquisition to date: WhatsApp. The decision, which cost Facebook $22 billion, is the biggest software-company acquisition that history has ever seen.

FACEBOOK AND ITS CHALLENGES

Facebook, the leading social-network platform, has over one billion active users on a monthly basis, while the acquired WhatsApp, a real-time-messaging service, records an average monthly active usage of 450 million. However, although statistically the Facebook network looks much stronger, when we break down the levels of activity within these two services, we can see there is a gap that Facebook needed to fill.

While Facebook had higher user numbers, much of the users were from limited regions, and Facebook was struggling to grow in places such as Europe, India, and Latin America. Moreover, the functions available to the users—such as instant messaging, uploading videos and photos, and voice messaging—were far less active than those of its future partner, WhatsApp. Much of this struggle stemmed from the fact that Facebook went public without any revenue from mobile devices.

The mobile-technology market was able to reach out to all age groups on a very personalized level, one that many of the Facebook's users complained that the social network lacked. In spite of mobile technology having limited features and capabilities, mobile-technology services have become the greatest competitors to the more traditional social-network services. Finally, relative to its competitors in the social-media business ecosystem, WhatsApp was a junior company and did not have a sufficient platform to battle with major players like Google, Microsoft, and Yahoo.

KEY FEATURES OF THE PARTNERSHIP

The partnership included these features:

- WhatsApp facilitated Facebook's plan to bringing "connectivity and utility to the world"(Facebook press release, Press: Tucker Bounds) through their mobile communication, which had already replaced the SMS communication.

- WhatsApp had one million users joining every day, making it the fastest growing company in terms of users. This rapid growth was an asset to Facebook.
- WhatsApp continued to operate in an independent fashion and retained its brand.
- WhatsApp's cofounder and CEO, Jan Koum, joined Facebook's board of directors.

PARTNERSHIP OUTCOME

The partnership experienced the following outcomes:

- It brought more connectivity and utility to the world by delivering more Internet services officially and affordably.
- WhatsApp gained 450 million users worldwide, with 70 percent of them active on any one day. The service has more than one million users being added every day.
- The WhatsApp deal gave Facebook a pathway for entering the crowded Chinese market.
- The acquisition of WhatsApp allowed Facebook to remain competitive and innovative, in line with its long-haul objectives, and secure its position as the market leader.

Twenty-Nine

Kraft and Heinz Merger

In July 2015, the successful merger between Kraft Foods Group and the H. J. Heinz Company was announced. The transaction formed the fifth-largest food and beverage company in the world and the third largest in North America. The Kraft-Heinz Group—with a combination of thirteen different brands, each valued at $500 million or more—was created by the Berkshire Hathaway and 3G Capital, with each owning a 25 percent stake.

CHALLENGES FOR KRAFT AND HEINZ

Prior to the merger, Heinz was generating 61 percent of its total sales from outside North America, while Kraft Foods was generating 98 percent of its total sales from North America alone. Although Kraft was very strong in its own segment, it was only reaching out to its confined region of North America and lacked the international presence of competitors such as Nestlé.

An ultimate goal of both brands was the increasing need to save commodity costs, manufacturing costs, and productivity costs in order to compete in a market in which consumer demand for packaged-food products was deteriorating.

KEY FEATURES OF THE PARTNERSHIP
The partnership included the following features:

- Heinz shareholders took a 51 percent stake in the newly formed company.
- Kraft shareholders took a one-time cash dividend of $16.50.
- There were approximate annual sales revenues of $28 billion.
- For an annual saving plan estimated at $1.5 billion, two thousand five hundred jobs were cut

- Leaders of the new company included Alex Behring (chairman of Heinz) as chairman; John Cahill (chairman & CEO of Kraft) as vice chairman; and Bernardo Hees (CEO of Heinz) as CEO.
- The merger enabled higher economies of scale in North America.
- The new company held dual headquarters in Pittsburgh and Chicago.
- The board of directors of the combined company consisted of five members appointed from the Kraft board, the current Heinz board, three members from Berkshire Hathaway, and three members from 3G Capital.

PARTNERSHIP OUTCOME

The partnership experienced the following outcomes:

- Kraft-Heinz was well served by its unparalleled portfolio of leading brands including five hundred million-plus labels which amounted to $8 billion worth in brands.
- The company was exposed to some of the sector's more attractive categories, such as baby food, cheese, and ketchup. In the meantime, the company maintained the biggest branded-food-service business in the United States.
- The merger created good cash flow; cash flow had been at its best level and was expecting to improve as new cost-cutting measures take hold.

- The department-to-capital ratio panned out to be more manageable.
- The company expects to see $1.5 billion in annual cost savings by the end of 2017.

Thirty

AOL and Time Warner Merger

January 10, 2000, marked the announcement of the merger between America Online (AOL) and Time Warner, a deal valued at $350 billion. The new AOL Time Warner would be the fourth-largest company in the United States, as measured by stock-market valuation, behind only Microsoft, General Electric, and computer-network maker Cisco Systems.

In early January at the time of the announcement of the merger between AOL and Time Warner, the market value of AOL was approximately $164 billion, while Time Warner's valuation was approximately $97 billion, making the combined companies one of the top-ten largest companies in the world.

REASON BEHIND THE MERGER

AOL was formed in 1985 as a quantum computer system, and after changing the name to AOL (from America Online) in 1991, AOL was and continued to be the world's largest Internet-service provider with an excess of twenty million customers. Between 1996 and 2000, AOL realized an 86 percent compound annual growth rate in revenue and 106 percent growth in stock price. AOL had twelve thousand employees and $4.8 billion in revenue.

Time Warner, however, was more established and far more complex. During 1996 to 2000, compound revenues and stock-price growth were 18 percent and 36 percent. Time Warner had seventy thousand employees and $26.8 billion in revenue.

The $190 billion in stock that AOL agreed to issue to acquire Time Warner made it the largest merger in the US history. Both sides agreed to offer significant brand recognition, including the following:

- AOL
- Warner Brothers
- HBO
- Netspace
- *Time*
- CNN
- TNT
- CompuServe
- Warner Music Group
- *Sports Illustrated*
- *Fortune*

Time Warner brought with it a broadband-distribution platform. This platform was then able to expand significantly with the AOL interactive market. The merger at that time had the potential to combine the power of the Internet with the world's most trusted information and entertainment brands.

Therefore the merger was to give AOL Time Warner a competitive advantage globally and allow it to expand its businesses and brands to international markets.

KEY FEATURES OF THE PARTNERSHIP

The partnership included these features:

- AOL would own 55 percent of the new company.
- Time Warner would own 45 percent of the new company.
- The new board would have an equal number of AOL and Time Warner directors.
- The two companies together employed eighty-two thousand people.
- AOL founder Steven Case would be chairman of the combined firm.
- AOL, in effect, converted a substantial portion of its paper value into control of real assets.
- Time Warner stockholders received a huge premium on the current market price of their stock.
- AOL had access to the thirteen million subscribers of the cable systems owned by Time Warner.
- The newly merged company had many industries that were blending together; broadband, cable modem, net access, digital cable television, and online music.

PARTNERSHIP OUTCOME

The AOL–Time Warner merger proved to be the biggest mistake in corporate history. Why did it fail?

The reasons behind the failure can be summarized as follows:

- Untested assumptions were taken as facts during the due-diligence process of evaluating organizational compatibility.
- Growth strategies were not executed.
- The boardroom and culture differences of AOL and Time Warner were never merged, and the integration only took place at the superficial corporate level.
- The vision was separated from the execution. The integration of the two companies was inadequately executed; many of the expected synergies between the two companies never actually materialized, due to the slowdown of advertisers and subscribers to

AOL–Time Warner services caused by the negative impact of September 11, 2001. This was escalated by the lack of collaboration within the merged company.

- Culture clash in the merged company created a heavy resistance in both executives and employees to implementing the growth strategy the company had put in place.
- The merger created negative financial synergy. In late 1990, the stock prices for the merged company were significantly overvalued. The stock prices of the merged company experienced an increase of 146 percent between the years 1996 and 2001, which provided it with an inflated market capitalization of $226 billion at the time of the merger.

This proved to be a problem, since the deal was stock for a stock merger; despite Time Warner having a higher annual turnover than AOL, it was still the smaller company by market value. Effectively the merger in practice was actually an acquisition.

On the other hand, in 2000, Time Warner was witnessing a fall in profits and a 14 percent reduction in share price, and by 2001 after the merger was finalized, the AOL-Time Warner bubble finally burst, leading to a severe reduction in value of the AOL division and losses reaching $99 billion. By the time of the dissolution of the merger in 2009, AOL's value was a mere $5.7 billion, and the total value of the two companies was one-seventh of their premerger prices.

Thirty-One

Vodafone Acquisition of Mannesmann

O n February 4, 2004, Mannesmann AG agreed to a take-over price of €190 billion by Vodafone; it was the largest take-over price ever paid until that date and still is among the highest. After tough negotiations, Germany's Mannesmann AG agreed to the take-over by Britain's Vodafone AirTouch, which was likely to re-shape the global telecommunications landscape. The deal married Britain's leading wireless player with the largest in Germany.

The transaction created the world's largest mobile-phone operator, with almost forty-two million customers in the United Kingdom, United States, Germany, Italy, France, and a host of other markets. The transaction was seen to have immediate impact in Europe, which was ahead of the United States in the development of wireless services.

REASON BEHIND THE ACQUISITION

The major reason behind the acquisition was to maintain a constant, healthy growth ratio over time. Through acquisitions, joint ventures, and strategic alliances, Vodafone had managed to control or participate in the majority of the mobile-phone services around the globe. Mannesmann was only one of many ventures that made the growth possible.

The following are other Vodafone adventures:

- 1999–2000: Mannesmann acquisition
- 2000–2002: China Mobile strategic alliance
- 2001–2003: SFR and Cegetel strategic alliance
- 2001–2003: Vodafone Spain acquisition of 17.8 percent of BT Spain
- 2004–2005: Vodafone Japan acquisition of Japan Telecom shares

Second, the acquisition would help expand the area of business. Mannesmann had the business in telecommunication equipment, Internet services, and hydraulic, material-handling, and plastics technology, as well as steel tubes. Vodafone would be able to enter into such areas without taking the risk of entrance.

Third, Mannesmann's big market share in Germany helped Vodafone to ensure leadership in the European market and even to become the biggest operator in the word. Finally the combination brought Vodafone big synergies from both revenue and cost-saving sides.

For example, Vodafone would greatly reduce the cost of the call from Germany to the United Kingdom as they were in the same system, and it attracted more users based on this kind of advantage. Besides the merger reduced the cost of purchasing. More investment in the overseas markets also reduced unsystematic risk and increased the value of the Vodafone brand.

KEY FEATURES OF THE PARTNERSHIP
The partnership included these features:

- Vodafone AirTouch continued to develop Mannesmann's wireless, wireline, and Internet strategies within the combined group.
- Düsseldorf was retained as one of two dual European headquarters with responsibility for Mannesmann's existing continental European mobile and fixed-line business.
- Mannesmann's telecommerce activities were integrated into Vodafone and developed.
- Vodafone AirTouch retained all existing facilities and activities in the Düsseldorf area and expanded activities, with particular emphases on data products and services.
- Vodafone reaffirmed its public statement of commitment to Mannesmann's employees.

- Vodafone AirTouch undertook the initial public offerings of the engineering and automotive business along the lines of Mannesmann's previously announced plans.
- Vodafone gave Mannesmann's shareholders 49.5 percent of the combined company's stock.
- The merger created a company with mobile-phone interests in fifteen European countries with thirty million customers.
- It was expected to generate savings of more than £1 billion by 2004.
- Worldwide the group would have the equivalent of forty-two million customers.
- The merger included a rate of 53.7 Vodafone shares for each share of Mannesmann stock.

PARTNERSHIP OUTCOME

A table to show the key performance comparison prior and post-merger

Key figures	Prior		Post
	Mannesmann (2000)	Vodafone (2000)	Vodafone (2012)
Turnover (in € mil)	23,265	13,069	54,578
EBITDA (in € mil)	4.3	5.2	17,031
Market cap (in € mil)	119,572	149,400	107,000

In addition to the table above, the partnership experienced the following outcomes:

- After the Mannesmann deal, the market cap of Vodafone became $365 billion (£228 billion), making it by far the largest company on the London stock market and the fourth largest in the world.
- Vodafone split off Mannesmann's engineering and automotive operations into a separate company.

Thirty-Two

Mars and Wrigley Acquisition

In April 2008, Mars, the makers of M&M's, announced a complete acquisition of Wm. Wrigley Jr., the chewing gum company, for a deal of $23 billion. Under this agreement, Wrigley became a separate stand-alone subsidiary of Mars with approximately $5.4 billion in sales. The strong cultural heritage of the two legendary American companies with their shared commitment to innovation and quality and their top-class global brands provided a great basis for this combination and great potential for developing growth.

Wrigley was the recognized leader in confections with a wide range of product offerings including gum, mints, hard and chewy candies, and chocolate. The company had global annual sales of approximately $5.4 billion and distributed its world-famous brands in more than 180 countries worldwide. Wrigley brands were Spearmint, Juicy Fruit, Altoids, Doublemint, Life Savers, Big Red, Boomer, and Pim Rom.

Mars was a family owned company that produced some of the world's leading confectionery, food, and pet-care products and had a growing beverage and health-nutrition business. Mars operated in more than sixty-six countries and employed more than forty-eight thousand associates worldwide. The company's global annual sales were reaching approximately $22 billion. Mars produced many world-famous, recognizable trademarks including Dover, Milky Way, M&M's, Snickers, Mars, Uncle Ben's rice, and the Royal Canin and Pedigree pet-care products.

REASON BEHIND THE ACQUISITION

The primary motives behind the acquisition were definitely the potential of operating synergy between the two firms, related diversifications, and a tremendous increase and creation of market power.

The merger was expected to affect operating savings by achieving economies of scale in manufacturing certain products and economies in scope by combining and eliminating sublimate functions. The new company ensured operational efficiency in combining marketing and distribution capabilities.

The new company achieved greater focus by concentrating on nonchocolate confectionery brands in Wrigley, while Mars achieved greater related diversification in nonchocolate products. The combined company got additional pricing power by increasing market share from 10 percent to 14 percent of the global confectionery market.

KEY FEATURES OF THE PARTNERSHIP

- Wrigley became a separate, stand-alone subsidiary of Mars.
- The deal, in which the maker of M&M's and Snickers bars bought the remaining 20 percent in the chewing-gum group held by Berkshire Hathaway, solidified Mars's leading position in the $177 billion global confectionery market.
- Berkshire, which received preference shares after paying a 5 percent annual dividend for the stake, also loaned the chocolate and pet-food company $4.4 billion, which has since been repaid.
- Mars and Wrigley together held a 13.5 percent share in the global confectionery market.
- Shareholders of Wrigley received eighty dollars in cash for each share of stock.
- In addition to Berkshire Hathaway, Goldman Sachs and JPMorgan Chase also provided financing for the deal.
- The Wrigley headquarters was maintained in Chicago, and Mars's non chocolate confectionery brands, including Starburst and Skittles, were transferred to Wrigley.
- William Wrigley Jr. remained executive chairman of Wrigley, reporting to Mars's global president, Paul Michaels.
- Between them, Mars and Wrigley employed sixty-four thousand people and generated global sales of $27 billion annually.

PARTNERSHIP OUTCOME

The partnership achieved the following outcomes:

- In addition to new product innovations, Wrigley and Mars Chocolate introduced several cobranded initiatives at the show, including The Candy Bowl program that built on the success of previous year's inaugural joint Super Bowl promotion.
- The companies also shared details on their merchandising tools and insights, which were already being implemented with more than eighteen thousand retailers and provided customized recommendations on strategic product placements to maximize sales.
- These collaborative initiatives reflected the recent announcement from parent company, Mars, Inc., about the intent to combine the chocolate and Wrigley segments to create Mars Wrigley Confectionery.
- The combination helped deliver greater value to customers and enable the segment to address consumer trends and insights holistically in what was increasingly seen as one global confections category.

Thirty-Three

Procter and Gamble Acquisition of Gillette

In early January 2005, Procter and Gamble (P&G), the consumer-products giant, announced their plans to acquire shaving powerhouse Gillette for stock initially valued at $54 billion.

The deal created the world's biggest consumer-products enterprise and was expected to strengthen P&G's influence against mass-market retailers like Wal-Mart Stores, Inc. The deal pushed the new company's revenue above $60 billion so that it surpassed Unilever, which had revenue of $53 billion, and it also pushed annual sales growth.

The combination brought together the marketing and distribution strength of Procter and Gamble, whose products were marketed largely to women, with Gillette's high-profile brands, which are marketed mainly to men. The only major areas of overlapping were in deodorants and oral care—predominantly in manual and power toothbrushes—but the merger helped P&G to enter one of the most attractive categories in personal care products.

Gillette and Procter and Gamble had almost the same history, culture, and core strength in branding, scale, innovation, and go-to-the-market capabilities, which made this merger a perfect one. As both companies faced low-sales problems, one innovative company acquired the other innovative company to enlarge its product line, and both of them emerged as winners after applying similar approaches.

REASON BEHIND THE MERGER

The merger brought a strong synergy and enlarged and strengthened the combined company's brand portfolio. After the merger, Gillette got more opportunity ties for selling its products in various developing markets, like China and Eastern Europe.

They were interested in improving and expanding their products and targets as much as possible in different consumer markets. The merger enabled the company to enlarge its product line and become the world's largest consumer-product company.

Gillette's core customer segment was men, while the core customers of P&G were women; thus the two companies complemented each other. Gillette was the market leader in several product categories, including blades, razors, oral care, and batteries; these categories were the target of P&G in order to complete their product line.

Gillette was a strong company in emerging markets, such as India and Brazil, whereby Procter and Gamble had been continuously outperformed by Unilever in these markets. Similarly Procter and Gamble was the leading company in the Chinese market; the merger enabled Gillette to sell its products in China and push the overall sales revenue significantly.

KEY FEATURES OF THE PARTNERSHIP
The partnership included these features:

- The deal created the world's biggest consumer-products enterprise.
- P&G offered 0.975 of its shares for each outstanding share of Gillette.
- P&G acquired all of Gillette's business, including manufacturing, technical, and other facilities.
- P&G and its subsidiaries bought back $18 billion to $22 billion of P&G's common stock the first twelve months after the merger.

PARTNERSHIP OUTCOME
The partnership experienced these outcomes:

- Procter and Gamble's acquisition of Gillette has supported the consumer good group by tripling the revenue versus the forecasted one in the second quarter after the acquisition
- Profits grew twenty nine percent ahead of expectations in the first year of acquisition versus the same period the year before.

- After the merger, both companies operated a successful cost-reduction plan, as they laid off 4 percent of the total combined workforce and integrated the headquarters and business operations. They also managed to retain the best employees from both companies. This resulted in larger profit margins in the short and long term.

Thirty-Four

Philip Morris
Acquisition of Nabisco
Holdings Corp.

In June 2000, Philip Morris, the owner of Kraft Foods, acquired Nabisco Holdings Corp. for $14.9 billion in cash. With the Nabisco purchase, Philip Morris's Kraft unit was able to retain its position as the second-largest food company in the world, after Nestlé.

The combined Kraft-Nabisco operation had a wide array of brands, from Cracker Barrel cheese and Maxwell House coffee to Ritz Crackers and A1 Steak Sauce, and thus commanded enviable leverage with retailers. The acquisition added more pressure on other food companies facing weak profit margins and low levels of sales and forced them to get bigger in order to be able to compete with large companies like Nestlé, Kraft Foods, and Unilever (the largest global food business).

Nabisco was an American manufacturer and snacks company with headquarters located in East Hanover, New Jersey, and its plant located in Chicago. Nabisco had a variety of products, including Chips Ahoy, BelVita, Oreos, Ritz Crackers and Wheat Thins. It distributed its products in the whole of the United States, United Kingdom, Mexico, and Venezuela, as well as other parts of South America.

According to the Philip Morris company, its history can be traced to Mr. Philip Morris's 1847 opening of a single shop selling tobacco and cigarettes on London's Bond Street. Philip Morris, headquartered in New York, was the world's largest tobacco company with its Marlboro, Benson & Hedges, and Parliament brands.

In 1999, Philip Morris launched its website and admitted that smoking can cause lung cancer and other diseases. While Philip Morris spent much of its effort cleaning up its tainted tobacco image, the company was making great progress in the food industry. From 1992 to 1997, Kraft's profit margin had increased to 16 percent—one of the highest in the food industry. The unit also accounted for 35 percent of the frozen-food market after the successful 1995 launch of DiGiorno Rising Crust Pizza.

REASON BEHIND THE ACQUISITION

With the Nabisco purchase, Kraft surpassed the combined Unilever-Best Foods food unit to regain its position as the second-largest food company in the world, behind Nestlé SA.

Importantly, it took Kraft food into the fast-growing snack-foods area, which was growing at twice the rate of the total food area. For Kraft, the acquisition also meant faster top-line growth, increased productivity, higher margins and acceler-ated earnings.

KEY FEATURES OF THE PARTNERSHIP

The partnership included these features:

- The deal added eighteen brands to the company's existing fifty-five brands.
- Philip Morris offered the public 20 percent of the stock in the newly combined food company.
- Kraft was managed as a separate subsidiary, and no Kraft assets or businesses were sold off to pay off the debt incurred.
- The deal was financed through $1.5 billion of Philip Morris's own cash and $12 billion in credit lines provided by New York's Citibank and sixty-three other US and foreign banks.
- The merger agreement called for Kraft shareholders to receive $106 per share in cash through a tender.
- The combined company had one hundred seventeen thousand employees in food operations.
- The combined company knocked Unilever, the British-Dutch company, out of first place as the world's largest producer of consumer goods.
- John M. Richman remained Kraft's chairman and also become a Philip Morris vice chairman.
- Michael A. Miles, Kraft's president and chief operating officer, remained president of Kraft, took on the

additional title of chief executive officer, and continued to report to John M. Richman.

- Kraft's name survived as a subsidiary of Philip Morris, while the Philip Morris parent company continued to operate as before.

PARTNERSHIP OUTCOME

The partnership experienced these outcomes:

- Synergies from the successful integration of acquired businesses into Kraft drove margin improvement.
- In 2004, Kraft generated more than $300 million in cumulative synergies from the Nabisco acquisition and a cumulative synergy total of $600 million by 2005.

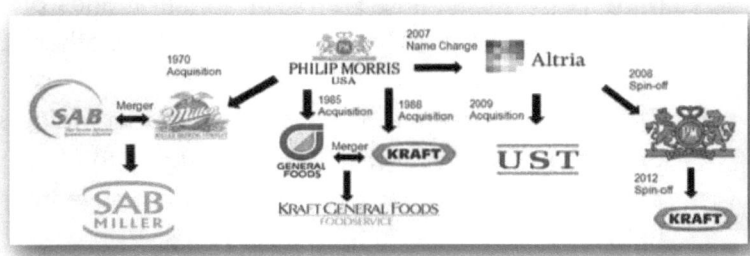

Thirty-Five

Kraft Foods and
Cadbury Acquisition

After long months of fiercely resisting any agreement, Cadbury agreed in January 2010 to be taken over and accepted the offer from Kraft Foods in a deal worth $19 billion. This deal gave Kraft Foods a greater opportunity to expand its footprint in many emerging markets in higher-growth sectors, like gum and candy. It also transformed the company's portfolio and accelerated long-term growth to ensure high potential returns. As for Cadbury, it benefited from the supply chain of a larger company and was able to be present in different markets and regions with the backup support from Kraft Food.

Cadbury was established in Birmingham, England, in 1824 by John Cadbury, who was dealing mainly in tea, coffee, and drinking chocolate. The company business was gradually developed by John's brother, Benjamin, followed by his son, Richard. Dairy Milk chocolate was introduced in 1905, and with steady development up until 1914, chocolate was the company's best-selling product. In 1919, Cadbury merged with J. S. Fry and Sons and with Schweppes in 1969. Cadbury was a constant constituent of the FTSE until the company was bought by Kraft Foods in 2010.

REASON BEHIND THE ACQUISITION
The merger enabled Kraft Foods to focus on growth categories. It aimed to be the leader in the snack, confectionery, and quick-meals categories. By integrating world-famous brands such as Kraft's Oreo Cookies, Velveeta Cheese, and Cadbury chocolate bars under one roof, the acquisition helped both companies to compete effectively against the giant rivals and to create a global food giant with approximately $50 billion in revenue a year.

The acquisition gave Kraft Foods an expanded footprint in developing markets by helping Kraft Foods to enlarge its geographical presence in developing markets like China, India, Mexico, and Russia. Kraft Foods expected to increase its market share in developing economies from 20 percent before the Cadbury acquisition to 26 percent post acquisition. Since Cadbury had a 70 percent market share in the Indian chocolate market and 1.2 million retail outlets, Kraft Foods got a solid presence in the second-fastest-growing economy, where large sections of Indians, including rural populations, had turned toward processed foods.

The acquisition also gave more value to shareholders; Kraft Foods was able to target long-term, organic growth in excess of 5 percent and sustainable, long-term EPS growth of approximately 11 percent. The higher the long-term growth rates in revenues and bottom lines driven by the synergy of both companies, the more value given to the company shareholders.

KEY FEATURES OF THE PARTNERSHIP

The partnership included these key features:

- Per-share price of £8.40 per share plus a special ten-pence-per-share dividend
- Overcoming of entry barriers in new markets
- Entrance to emerging markets through cross-border acquisitions, such as Brazil, South Africa, India, China, and Mexico. Cadbury allowed cross-border acquisition into growing regions, such as Africa, Asia, and the Middle East.
- Increased presence in the gum market, which had the highest growth rate in the confectionery market. Cadbury was the market leader with a 29 percent share, compared to Kraft's 0.1 percent.
- Accumulated portfolio of more than forty confectionery brands
- Integration of human resources, including job redundancies and changes to compensation packages
- Potential for the synergy of revenues over time from investments in marketing, distribution, and product development

PARTNERSHIP OUTCOME

The partnership experienced the following outcomes:

- A year after the acquisition, the firm announced a further two hundred job cuts but also £50 million in investment.
- In 2012, an additional $250 million in costs was cut from general and administrative expenses.

Thirty-Six

Nestlé and Gerber Acquisition

In April 2007, Nestlé, the Swiss-based food company, announced the agreement of Novartis pharmaceutical company to acquire Gerber, the food line of Novartis. Through the transaction, Nestlé acquired sole control over the whole Gerber business.

Gerber was wholly owned by Novartis, a major producer for health-care products. The company was active in the manufacturing, marketing, and sales of baby food, baby-care products, and baby accessories as well as the life-insurance business.

Nestlé was mainly active in the production, marketing, and sales of large varieties of food and beverage products, including products for the nutrition of infants, such as formula, cereals, and meals.

REASON BEHIND THE ACQUISITION

The merger widened the combined company's geographic potential. Gerber's geographic presence was in the United States, while in Europe, it had a production facility solely in Poland and achieved only 3 percent of its global turnover from Europe. Nestlé, however, had products that are more widely spread in Europe, especially Western Europe; therefore, both companies' activities complemented each other in terms of geography and products.

The merger had a conglomerate-benefits effect. In addition to the strength of the portfolio, the post-merger effect has to be considered in the context of the new company's relative strength in comparison to its competitor brands and portfolios. Nestlé became a full-range supplier in not only the baby-food line but also other strong food brands, like Nescafé and Nesquik. Therefore it used its new portfolio power to compete effectively with any other food-producing competitors. It also prevented new entry or impede the expansion of existing single-brand competitors.

After the acquisition, Nestlé used its financial and portfolio power to limit the access of competitors to distribution channels and reduce shelf space. Since Nestlé was the producer of many must-have brands, it could afford to be a tough negotiator with retailers in order to get better terms and conditions. The acquisition also gave the ability for Nestlé to be a full-range supplier of baby-food products without changing the overall competitive environment and organism.

Overall the mergers made possible the strategic use of the portfolio combination and financial leverage.

KEY FEATURES OF THE PARTNERSHIP

The partnership included these features:

- The acquisition of Gerber, which came in the wake of the Jenny Craig and Novartis Medical Nutrition purchases, allowed access to the group's global R&D network to drive innovation.
- The acquisition of Gerber, which commanded some 82 percent of the US baby-food market, also constituted a decisive step toward establishing Nestlé Nutrition as the undisputed global leader in the nutrition field, with annual sales of around CHF 10 billion and covering all important sectors like infant formula, baby food, medical nutrition, and weight management.
- The deal generated cost savings of approximately $95 million, or 5 percent of sales, by 2011.
- With the merger, four thousand five hundred Gerber employees joined the group.
- The sale marked the end of Novartis's campaign to sell off non-health-care-related operations and a transition to a group focused 100 percent on the health-care business.
- Gerber added three hundred food items for babies and infants, plus baby-care products.

PARTNERSHIP OUTCOME

The partnership experienced these outcomes:

- Nestlé 2016 held the largest share of the global baby-food market.

- Nestlé managed to expand the brand name of Gerber and feature it in all major European countries.

Thirty-Seven

PepsiCo and Tropicana Acquisition

In July 1998, PepsiCo Inc. announced their acquisition of Tropicana juice company from Seagram's for $3.3 billion in cash. The deal united the world's second beverage company with the largest producer of branded juices and set up another dimension to the battle between PepsiCo and Coca-Cola.

Tropicana, with nearly $2 billion in revenue during 1997, produced and distributed Pure Premium, Season's Best and Dole line of juice products. Analysts confirmed that both companies should fit well together as they both sold most of their products through grocery stores. With this deal, Tropicana expanded PepsiCo's presence in the $16 billion US juice market. It also boosted the company presence in the morning, when consumption of PepsiCo's traditional carbonated soft drinks was relatively low.

Founded in 1947 by Anthony Rossi in Bradenton, Florida, Tropicana was an American multinational company that primarily made fruit-based beverages. It worked with more than twelve established Florida groves, which were selected for sandy soil conditions and advanced irrigation practices.

PepsiCo Inc. was an American multinational food, snack, and beverage corporation formed in 1965. After the merger with Frito-Lay Inc., PepsiCo expanded from its namesake product, Pepsi, to a broader range of food and beverage brands, the largest of which included the acquisition of Tropicana products in 1998.

REASON BEHIND THE ACQUISITION

Tropicana had a strong lead in the fresh-beverage part of the juice business. The company produced, pasteurized, and packaged the juice and turned it into concentrate. As a result, Tropicana had a 72 percent market share in that highly profitable segment.

The deal brought together the world's second-biggest beverage company with the largest producer of branded juices and thus gave a competitive edge to the battle between PepsiCo and Coca-Cola Co.

Tropicana had 44 percent of the market for chilled orange juice. And after years of growth, the soft-drink industry in the United States was nearly flat. The big battle was over the products without fizz, and PepsiCo was moving ahead on a number of fronts.

Outside the United States, Tropicana held leading positions in the chilled-orange-juice industries in Belgium, Canada, France, and the United Kingdom. The company also had expanding businesses in Japan, China, Taiwan, and Hong Kong.

KEY FEATURES OF THE PARTNERSHIP

- Eric J. Foss led the newly combined bottling operations, called Pepsi Beverages Company (PBC), and Massimo F. d'Amore continued to lead Tropicana, and Latin American beverages as CEO of PepsiCo Beverages Americas (PBA).
- Gary M. Rodkin, president of Tropicana's North American business, became president and chief executive of the juice business.
- Tropicana operated as a division separate from PepsiCo.

PARTNERSHIP OUTCOME

The partnership experienced these outcomes:

- The beverage innovation team at PepsiCo entered into the consumer demand for healthier drinks.
- Under the Tropicana brand, the company expanded the Farmstand fruit and vegetable juice line with a tropical green flavor.
- The new products came during an era when the beverage industry faced accumulative pressure from consumers and public officials regarding the calorie and sugar content of ingredients in soft drinks.

KEY PERFORMANCE PRIOR AND POST-ACQUISITION

	1998	1997
Net sales	$23,674	$22,851
Income from continuing operations	$1,939	$1,427
Income per share from continuing operations	$1.28	$0.91

Thirty-Eight

Adidas acquisition of Reebok

In April 2005, Adidas, the Germany-based global power, announced a $3.8 billion deal to acquire Canton, Massachusetts–based Reebok. This united two of the world's top sport companies and created a much stronger new identity.

The Adidas-Reebok combination had a strong, influential power with suppliers in securing shelf space at retail outlets, in bidding for sponsorships and endorsements, and in demanding discounts on its mass-media advertising plans. The deal filled holes in each company's shoe portfolio; Reebok was strong in tennis shoes, fitness, and basketball, while Adidas had a grip on football and team sports.

REASON BEHIND THE ACQUISITION

The acquisition of Reebok by Adidas had many reasons and advantages for both companies. The brand names did not change and were not made into one single identity, as per the strategy of the new alliance. This allowed the two brands to continue performing and targeting different market segments.

The acquisition led to the overlapping operations in the areas of athletic goods, like sportswear, apparel, and sporting goods. Thus both companies were able to manufacture the goods and apparel with minimal fixed and variable costs. The manufacturing time of the goods was decreased dramatically, with the combination of streamlined operations.

Each company was proficient in manufacturing techniques, and hence it was helpful for both of the companies with different brands to produce wide variations of sporting goods, equipment, and apparel. Patents were shared among the companies so that upper- and middle-level products could be manufactured with the same patent.

Both companies exchanged their technological expertise to optimize the manufacturing process. Expertise in operations, human-resource management, and financial-transaction management were able to be exchanged; Adidas was good at manufacturing sports apparel, while Reebok was more advanced in producing sports equipment.

The acquisition achieved significant cost cutting in both companies since both companies were able to share common marketing strategies, manufacturing processes, and financial operations. Both companies benefited from the exchange of employees based on experience and qualifications, which allowed both companies to eliminate the hiring of a new workforce and thus reduce costs.

The acquisition also affected the companies' presence in emerging markets, as it led to the capture of business opportunities and enlarging market share. It allowed both companies to have a stronger presence and market share in the United States, where Nike was very strong. Adidas, with the support of Reebok, was able to excel in performance and reach rival Nike in these regions. Similarly with the support of Adidas, Reebok was able to have more presence in the Asian continent.

KEY FEATURES OF THE PARTNERSHIP
The partnership included these features:

- Shared R&D, patents, technology, and innovations
- Increase in product line
- Acclivity in market share
- Coverage of both upper- and middle-priced markets
- Cross-over promotion by sponsored athletes
- Ramping up of sales and marketing efforts. It reduced reliance on low-traffic, shopping-mall-based outlets and placed Reebok apparel and footwear in higher-end department stores and larger sporting-goods ventures.
- Closure of factories in Indonesia
- Reebok brand repositioning in order to widen its appeal

PARTNERSHIP OUTCOME
The partnership experienced these outcomes:

- Reebok's acquisition by Adidas may have contributed to Reebok's increase in customer satisfaction, as the combined brands led to a near doubling of US sales, rivalling Nike in market share.

- In an endeavor to differentiate itself from the competition, each company developed exclusive relationships with highly distinguished organizations and individuals.
- Reebok had the exclusive rights to market its products for the NBA, NHL, NFL, and the WNBA.
- Adidas obtained contracts with professional European soccer clubs such as Chelsea, Bayern Munich, Real Madrid, and A. C. Milan. On the other hand, without an established superstar, Nike's endorsements lacked the influence they once held with the likes of Michael Jordan.

Thirty-Nine

Coca-Cola and Glacéau
Vitaminwater Acquisition

I n May 2007, Coca-Cola announced the take-over of Glacéau, the maker of Vitaminwater, for $4.2 billion in cash. This take-over which was expected in order for Coca-Cola to upgrade its portfolio of noncarbonated beverages. Noncarbonated-beverages sale volume had been growing much faster than soda in the United States, and thus such an acquisition was considered a potential game changer in the market of non-carbonated drinks.

REASONS BEHIND THE ACQUISITION
Glacéau's high-quality growth as well as a strong pipeline of innovative products and brands with increasing demand allowed Coca-Cola to stand stronger in front of PepsiCo and to solicit larger market share in energy drinks.

The acquisition provided Coca-Cola with a strong foundation from which to develop active-lifestyle beverages and ensured immediate, high-quality growth for the entire company.

The merger upgraded Coca-Cola's portfolio of noncarbonated beverages, the sales of which had been growing much faster than soda in the United States in recent years.

KEY FEATURES OF THE PARTNERSHIP
The partnership included the following features:

- Coca-Cola took full ownership of Glacéau.
- The Tata stake (multinational Indian Holding company – who owned 30 percent of Glacéau) was acquired later than the majority stake. Tata got $1.2 billion of the $4.1 billion purchase price.
- The acquisition of Glacéau expanded Coca-Cola's ability to meet consumer needs across the entire spectrum of sparkling and still beverages.
- Glacéau operated as a separate business unit within Coca-Cola North America (CCNA). This structure

allowed Glacéau to continue to maximize its focus, speed, sales, and execution capabilities, while leveraging the scale of CCNA's resources in supply chain, marketing and consumer insights, large-customer management, and food service.

- Glacéau with its brands also provided Coca-Cola with highly attractive longer-term international opportunities.
- Coca-Cola made a cash payment of approximately $2.9 billion for a 71.4 percent interest in Glacéau and entered into a put and call option agreement with certain entities associated with the Tata Group to acquire the remaining 28.6 percent ownership interest in Glacéau.

PARTNERSHIP OUTCOME

The partnership experienced the following outcomes:

- On October 22, 2007, Coca-Cola exercised its right to call the remaining interest in Glacéau and paid Tata $1.2 billion; as a result, Coca-Cola owned 100 percent of Glacéau as of December 31, 2007.
- The years subsequent to the Vitaminwater purchase saw Coca-Cola's marketing team do wonders; Vitaminwater went from annual sales of $350 million to more than $1 billion.
- The acquisition of Glacéau expanded Coca-Cola's ability to meet consumer needs further across the entire spectrum of sparkling and still beverages.
- Vitamin water, smart water, fruit water and vitamin energy brands, Glacéau have uniquely positioned in

key market categories, with a leading position in enhanced water brands and energy drinks. These categories have made up a large portion of the beverage industry's volume and gross profit growth in North America through 2010.

- As Glacéau operated as a separate business unit within Coca-Cola, it allowed them to successfully continue to win in the marketplace by maximizing its focus, speed, sales and execution capabilities, while leveraging the scale of Coca-Cola North America's resources supply chain, marketing and consumer insights, large customer management and food services.

Forty

Microsoft's Acquisition
of Nokia

In September 2013, Microsoft made a surprise announcement that the company had concluded the acquisition of Nokia smartphone business for a deal of $7.2 billion. This the biggest acquisition in Microsoft's history.

The Nokia name came from the Nokia town and the Nokianvirta River. The Nokia company history started in 1865, when mining engineer Fredrick Idestam established a groundwood pulp mill on the banks of the Tammerkoski rapids in the town of Tampere, in southwestern Finland.

Microsoft is an American multinational technology company, headquartered in Washington DC. Microsoft develops, manufactures, licenses, supports and sells computer software, consumer electronics and personal computers and is best known for software products Microsoft Windows line of operating systems. Microsoft was founded by Paul Allen and Bill Gates during April 1975 to develop and sell basic interpreters for Altair 8800. It rose to dominate the personal computer operating system market with MS-DOS.

REASON BEHIND THE ACQUISITION

The acquisition enabled Microsoft to keep its momentum. Industry figures, at the time of the acquisition, showed Microsoft's Windows 8 phone posting its highest-ever market share (8.3 percent across the United Kingdom, Germany, France, Italy, and Spain), allowing the mobile OS to leapfrog Blackberry and become the third most popular mobile operating system globally.

As 81 percent of all Windows phone sales came from Nokia hardware, Microsoft decided to acquire Nokia's resources.

The partnership's direct control means better integration of handsets with the Windows phone. By unifying the hardware and software, they were able to keep the production of both hardware and software within the same company. This benefited the developers by reducing OS fragmentation and creating consistent hardware specifications. It boosted the OS security by encouraging users to update to the latest version of the software, leading to greater trust in the brand.

Midrange devices, such as the 520, were great in attracting first-time smartphone users; the handsets were reasonably priced and durable, and the Windows 8 phones were optimized to work fluidly, even on lower-spec hardware. The design language of colorful contrasts, titles, and fonts worked in a low-resolution screen.

More importantly, the purchase of the larger Nokia brand was perfect for targeting the next billions of users accessing the Internet. The Microsoft purchase also included a ten-year license to use the network Nokia brand on failure phones, and by maintaining the Finnish manufacturer's high standards, Microsoft expected to have an easier task of convincing consumers to shift to the Windows phone ecosystem over the next decade.

KEY FEATURES OF THE PARTNERSHIP
The partnership included these features:

- Microsoft built a data center in Finland.
- Tami Reller and Mark Penn headed all Microsoft and Nokia's global marketing.
- Microsoft acquired Nokia's mobile-phones and smart-devices business units, including Nokia's design team and its operations; all related production facilities, sales, and marketing functions; and related activities.
- In total, Nokia transferred thirty-two thousand employees to Microsoft, of whom four thousand seven hundred were in Finland.
- Microsoft inherited Nokia's Herec cloud-based mapping platform, which provided global positioning services to Microsoft's Bing search engine, as well as

location devices for Garmin, BMW, Oracle, Amazon, and Yahoo.

- Nokia retains its solutions and networks division and a large number of its patents.
- Nokia's mapping entity was considered a separate business and wasn't included as part of the deal, but Microsoft agreed to a ten-year licensing agreement.
- Microsoft controlled IP agreements and any third-party contracts related to Nokia's devices.
- Nokia's imaging talent switched over to Microsoft.
- Stephen Elop, who served as Nokia's president and CEO, became the executive vice president of Microsoft's devices group and reported directly to CEO Satya Nadella.
- Microsoft continued to support Nokia's entire portfolio.

PARTNERSHIP OUTCOME

The partnership experienced the following outcomes:

- In July 2014, Microsoft cut eighteen thousand jobs primarily in the recently acquired Nokia business. After the acquisition, the company immediately began to restructure the Nokia business.
- Microsoft sold its feature phone assets to a subsidiary of Taiwanese firm Foxconn Technology and HMD Global (newly established firm at the time of acquisition) for $350 million in a move that allowed Nokia devices return to the market.

- Microsoft signed a licensing agreement with Nokia Technologies, Nokia's licensing unit, that gives HMD the sole use of the Nokia brand on mobile phones and tablets worldwide for the next decade (post-acquisition), as well as key cellular patents.
- All of these deals made HMD the sole global licensee for all types of Nokia-branded mobile phones and tablets
- The sale by Microsoft marked a further pullback from its mobile-phone business, one of the struggling areas of the company, since it purchased Nokia's mobile device unit in 2014 for $7.2 billion. The Windows Phone had just a 2.2 percent market share globally in 2015.

Forty-One

Royal Bank of Scotland Consortium Acquisition of ABN AMRO

In April 2007, the European Commission ordered Dutch regulators to allow the take-over of ABN AMRO by the Royal Bank of Scotland consortium in a deal worth $100 billion. This take-over is considered to be the world's biggest banking transaction ever, and it was the first cross-border take-over of a European bank.

Ranked as the eighth-largest bank in Europe, ABN AMRO had a significant presence in the European banking market with a huge organization of offices and representations in fifty-three countries. The bank was founded in 1824, and it had its headquarters in Amsterdam, with more than four thousand five hundred branches in fifty-three countries. It had more than one hundred five thousand employees before the take-over, and total operating income was reaching approximately $22.6 billion.

Royal Bank of Scotland is a commercial bank based in Edinburgh, Scotland with a history dating to the 17th century.

It was the 5th bank to survive in the United Kingdom and the only commercial institution created by the parliament of Scotland to remain in existence. It was one of the first banks in Europe to print its banknotes, and continued to print its own sterling banknotes under legal arrangements which allowed banks to issue currencies. Royal Bank of Scotland has been a subsidiary of the Lloyds banking group science Jan 2009.

REASONS BEHIND ROYAL BANK OF SCOTLAND ACQUISITION OF ABN AMRO BANK

1-Significant presence in the European banking market with a huge number of branches and offices in 55 countries.

2-The combined force of ABN Amro and Royal bank of Scotland allowed the new Owners of ABN to move up into the league of some of their American counterparts.

3-Royal bank of Scotland were able to access ABN's new group of clients particularly in the field where ABN held strong positions, for example in debt and risk management products.

4-Achieving economies of scale and huge cost savings as predicted during the RBS due diligence process (a process in which a potential acquirer instructs specialists to analyze the assets of the target organization and investigate further areas if required), RBS had forecast cost savings and revenue benefits of approx. 1.8 billion Euro.

KEY FEATURES OF THE PARTNERSHIP
The partnership included these features:

- On September 22, 2008, RFS Holdings became the sole shareholder in ABN AMRO.
- Holders of ABN AMRO ordinary shares received for each ABN AMRO ordinary share €35.60 in cash and 0.296 newly issued ordinary shares with a nominal value of twenty-five pence per share of RBS.
- The breakup of ABN involved four thousand five hundred branches across fifty-three countries and unravelling businesses ranging from cash-management operations in Asia to retail banking in Brazil.
- RBS took its wholesale and investment banking business and its Asian operations, while Santander got ABN's Italian and Brazilian units and Fortis its Dutch business and wealth- and asset-management operations.
- Business units in the Netherlands, asset management, and private banking were acquired by Fortis.
- The transfer of Banco Real (Brazil) and Antonveneta (Italy) was allocated to Santander.
- Business and client activities in Asia, Europe, and North America were transferred to RBS.
- In order to obtain clearance from the European Commission, some parts of the Fortis-acquired Business Unit Netherlands of ABN AMRO would be sold off.
- Fortis sold its subsidiary businesses of Hollandsche Bank-Unie and IFN Finance, two corporate-client business units, and thirteen district offices.

PARTNERSHIP OUTCOME

The partnership experienced the following outcomes:

- On October 1, 2007, Bank of America acquired LaSalle Bank Corp. (an indirect subsidiary of Netherlands-based ABN AMRO).
- This left the Edinburgh-based RBS with an under-achieving London-based investment banking franchise and some small-scale Asian operations.
- In 2008, the Belgian-Dutch bank Fortis was nationalized by the Dutch government to avert a liquidity crisis.

REASON BEHIND THE ACQUISITION'S FAILURE

The ABN AMRO acquisition took place with inadequate due diligence, and the acquisition failed.

The acquisition failed in part because of significant weaknesses in the Royal Bank of Scotland's capital position, as a result of management decisions and permitted by an inadequate global, regulatory capital framework.

Also there was overreliance on risky, short-term, whole-sale funding, which was permanently tied by an inadequate approach to the regulation of liquidity, as well as concerns and uncertainties about the Royal Bank of Scotland's underlying asset quality because of little fundamental analysis by the FSA.

Substantial losses in credit-training activities eroded market confidence. Both the bank and the regulator underestimated how bad the losses were. The Royal Bank of Scotland was mired in an overall systemic crisis, and the bank was in its worse relative position and extremely vulnerable to failure. Finally the underlying deficiencies in Royal Bank of Scotland's management, governance, and culture made it prone to poor decision-making.

Forty-Two

Conclusions About Mergers and Acquisitions

A fter going through mergers and acquisitions in various fields, it was seen that many companies find that the best way to get ahead and move further is to expand ownership boundaries through mergers and acquisitions. For others, separating the public-ownership subsidiary or benefits segment offers more advantages, at least in theory. Mergers create synergies and economies of scale, expand operations, and cut costs. Investors can take comfort in the idea that mergers will deliver enhanced market power.

By contrast, demerged companies often enjoy improved operating performance. Additional capital can fund growth organically or through acquisition; meanwhile investors benefit from the improved formation flow from the demerged companies.

Mergers and acquisitions come in all shapes and sizes; investors need to consider the complex issues involved in such transactions. We can learn the following.

A merger can take place when two companies decide to combine into one entity or when one company buys another. An acquisition always involves the purchase of one company by another.

The function of synergy allows for the enhanced cost efficiency of a new entity made from two smaller ones. Synergy is the logic behind mergers and acquisitions.

Acquiring companies use various methods to value their targets. Some of these methods are based on comparative ratios, such as price earnings and market value per share earnings; replacement costs; or discounted-cash-flow analysis.

A merger or acquisition deal can be executed by means of cash transaction, stock-for-stock transaction, or a combination of both.

Breakup or demerging strategies can provide companies with opportunities for raising additional equity funds, unlocking hidden shareholder value, and sharpening management focus.

Mergers can fail for many reasons, including lack of management foresight, the inability to overcome particular challenges, and loss of revenue momentum from neglect of day-to-day operations.

The current business world no longer allows room for stand-alone companies to perform, due to severe competition as well as the fact that the corporate market is being dominated by very few, giant corporations able to dictate control and direct the global economy.

About the Author

Ashraf Haggag is a senior executive with nearly three decades of experience in close proximity to the corporate market. His more recent experience has also taken him to every facet of the hospitality industry, where he has been exposed to a host of business features essential to a successful company.

His success in multiple business functions—including sales, marketing, revenue management, and administration—has allowed him to formulate his own thoughts and plans based on the idea that companies must work to produce new market zones in order to compete successfully.

www.ingramcontent.com/pod-product-compliance
Lightning Source LLC
Chambersburg PA
CBHW021405170526
45164CB00002B/516